my World
Social Studies®

Making Our Way

SAVVAS
LEARNING COMPANY

Copyright © 2013 by Savvas Learning Company LLC. All Rights Reserved. Printed in the United States of America.

This publication is protected by copyright, and permission should be obtained from the publisher prior to any prohibited reproduction, storage in a retrieval system, or transmission in any form or by any means, electronic, mechanical, photocopying, recording, or otherwise. For information regarding permissions, request forms, and the appropriate contacts within the Savvas Learning Company Rights Management group, please send your query to the address below.

Savvas Learning Company LLC, 15 East Midland Avenue, Paramus, NJ 07652

Attributions of third party content appear on pages R22–R23, which constitute an extension of this copyright page.

Savvas™ and **Savvas Learning Company™** are the exclusive trademarks of Savvas Learning Company LLC in the U.S. and other countries.

Savvas Learning Company publishes through its famous imprints **Prentice Hall®** and **Scott Foresman®** which are exclusive registered trademarks owned by Savvas Learning Company LLC in the U.S. and/or other countries.

myWorld Social Studies® and **Savvas Realize™** are exclusive trademarks of Savvas Learning Company LLC in the U.S. and/or other countries.

Unless otherwise indicated herein, any third party trademarks that may appear in this work are the property of their respective owners, and any references to third party trademarks, logos, or other trade dress are for demonstrative or descriptive purposes only. Such references are not intended to imply any sponsorship, endorsement, authorization, or promotion of Savvas Learning Company products by the owners of such marks, or any relationship between the owner and Savvas Learning Company LLC or its authors, licensees, or distributors.

ISBN-13: 978-0-328-63916-8
ISBN-10: 0-328-63916-8

28 21

Program Consulting Authors

The Colonial Williamsburg Foundation
Williamsburg, Virginia

Dr. Linda Bennett
Associate Professor, Department of Learning, Teaching, & Curriculum
College of Education
University of Missouri
Columbia, MO

Dr. Jim Cummins
Professor of Curriculum, Teaching, and Learning
Ontario Institute for Studies in Education
University of Toronto
Toronto, Ontario

Dr. James B. Kracht
Byrne Chair for Student Success
Executive Associate Dean
College of Education and Human Development
Texas A&M University
College Station, Texas

Dr. Alfred Tatum
Associate Professor, Director of the UIC Reading Clinic
Literacy, Language, and Culture Program
University of Illinois at Chicago
Chicago, IL

Dr. William E. White
Vice President for Productions, Publications and Learning Ventures
The Colonial Williamsburg Foundation
Williamsburg, VA

Consultants and Reviewers

PROGRAM CONSULTANT

Dr. Grant Wiggins
Coauthor, *Understanding by Design*

ACADEMIC REVIEWERS

Bob Sandman
Adjunct Assistant Professor of Business and Economics
Wilmington College–Cincinnati Branches
Blue Ash, OH

Jeanette Menendez
Reading Coach
Doral Academy Elementary
Miami, FL

Kathy T. Glass
Author, *Lesson Design for Differentiated Instruction*
President, Glass Educational Consulting
Woodside, CA

Roberta Logan
African Studies Specialist
Retired, Boston Public Schools/ Mission Hill School
Boston, MA

PROGRAM TEACHER REVIEWERS

Glenda Alford-Atkins
Eglin Elementary School
Eglin AFB, FL

Andrea Baerwald
Boise, ID

Ernest Andrew Brewer
Assistant Professor
Florida Atlantic University
Jupiter, FL

Riley D. Browning
Gilbert Middle School
Gilbert, WV

Charity L. Carr
Stroudsburg Area School District
Stroudsburg, PA

Jane M. Davis
Marion County Public Schools
Ocala, FL

Stacy Ann Figueroa, M.B.A.
Wyndham Lakes Elementary
Orlando, FL

LaBrenica Harris
John Herbert Phillips Academy
Birmingham, AL

Marybeth A. McGuire
Warwick School Department
Warwick, RI

Marianne Mack
Union Ridge Elementary
Ridgefield, WA

Emily L. Manigault
Richland School District #2
Columbia, SC

Laura Pahr
Holmes Elementary
Chicago, IL

Jennifer Palmer
Shady Hills Elementary
Spring Hill, FL

Diana E. Rizo
Miami-Dade County Public Schools/Miami Dade College
Miami, FL

Kyle Roach
Amherst Elementary, Knox County Schools
Knoxville, TN

Eretta Rose
MacMillan Elementary School
Montgomery, AL

Nancy Thornblad
Millard Public Schools
Omaha, NE

Jennifer Transue
Northampton, PA

Megan Zavernik
Howard-Suamico School District
Green Bay, WI

Dennise G. Zobel
Pittsford Schools–Allen Creek
Rochester, NY

Social Studies Handbook

My School, My Community

 How do people best cooperate?

Work in the Community

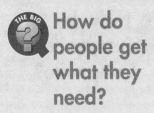

THE BIG **How do people get what they need?**

Looking at Our World

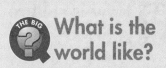 **What is the world like?**

Traditions We Share

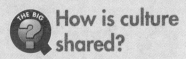

How is culture shared?

Our Past, Our Present

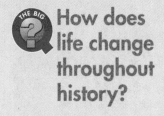

THE BIG ? **How does life change throughout history?**

Fact and Opinion

Fact = It is raining.

Opinion = Rainy days are fun!

Cause and Effect

Cause   Effect

Main Idea and Details

Main Idea

Details

Compare and Contrast

Sequence

The Writing Process

Good writers follow steps when they write. Here are five steps that will help you become a good writer!

Prewrite	Plan your writing.
Draft	Write your first draft.
Revise	Make your writing better.
Edit	Check your writing.
Share	Share your writing with others.

21st Century Learning Online Tutor

You can go online to myworldsocialstudies.com to practice the skills listed below. These are skills that will be important to you throughout your life. After you complete each skill tutorial online, check it off here in your worktext.

⦿ Target Reading Skills

- ☐ Main Idea and Details
- ☐ Cause and Effect
- ☐ Classify and Categorize
- ☐ Fact and Opinion
- ☐ Draw Conclusions
- ☐ Generalize
- ☐ Compare and Contrast
- ☐ Sequence
- ☐ Summarize

Collaboration and Creativity Skills

- ☐ Solve Problems
- ☐ Work in Cooperative Teams
- ☐ Resolve Conflict
- ☐ Generate New Ideas

Graph Skills

- ☐ Interpret Graphs
- ☐ Create Charts
- ☐ Interpret Timelines

Map Skills

- ☐ Use Longitude and Latitude
- ☐ Interpret Physical Maps
- ☐ Interpret Economic Data on Maps
- ☐ Interpret Cultural Data on Maps

Critical Thinking Skills

- ☐ Compare Viewpoints
- ☐ Use Primary and Secondary Sources
- ☐ Identify Bias
- ☐ Make Decisions
- ☐ Predict Consequences

Media and Technology Skills

- ☐ Conduct Research
- ☐ Use the Internet Safely
- ☐ Analyze Images
- ☐ Evaluate Media Content
- ☐ Deliver an Effective Presentation

My School, My Community

 How do people best cooperate?

Draw a picture of yourself being a good citizen in school.

my Story Video

 Begin With a Song

You're a Grand Old Flag

by George M. Cohan

You're a grand old flag,

You're a high flying flag

And forever in peace may you wave.

You're the emblem of the land I love,

The home of the free and the brave.

Vocabulary Preview

citizen

responsibility

right

vote

law

(Circle) examples of these words in the picture.

leader

government

governor

president

symbol

I Am a Good Citizen

Envision It!

Circle someone who is being helpful.

A **citizen** is a person who belongs to a state or country. Good citizens work to make things better. They help others. They follow rules. These are responsibilities of good citizens. A **responsibility** is something you should do.

1. ◎ **Fact and Opinion** <u>Underline</u> facts above that tell about good citizens.

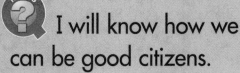
Vocabulary

citizen
responsibility
community

Citizens at School

You can be a good citizen at school. You can help others. You can follow rules. You can work well in groups.

Good citizens care about our country. We show this when we say the Pledge of Allegiance. The Pledge says we will be true to our country.

2. **Write** one way you can be a good citizen at school.

Citizens in the Community

A **community** is the place where people live, work, and play. You can be a good citizen in your community. You can follow community rules. You can do things that help others. You can help keep the community clean.

3. **Underline** ways above that tell how to be a good citizen in your community.

Picking up roadside litter

4. ⊙ **Main Idea and Details Read** the sentences below. **Underline** the main idea.

I am a good citizen. I follow the rules. I put trash where it should go.

5. I am a good citizen in the classroom when I

⬜ **Stop!** I need help with _____

▶ **Go!** Now I know _____

Envision It!

These children are helping at home.

Good citizens have rights and responsibilities. A **right** is what you are free to do or have. A responsibility is a thing you should do.

1. **Look** at the picture. What responsibility does the girl have?

_____

_____

_____

18

Draw one way you can help at home.

Vocabulary

right

cooperate

My Rights

You have rights at home and at school. You have the right to speak up. You have the right to belong to a group. You also have the right to laugh, talk, and play.

2. ◉ **Main Idea and Details** (Circle) the main idea above. **Underline** the detail sentences.

My Responsibilities

You have responsibilities at home. One may be to keep your room clean. Others may be to do your homework and to always tell the truth.

You have responsibilities at school. One is to do your best work. Others are to follow rules and take turns.

3. **Mark** the boxes that show your responsibilities.

My Responsibilities

At Home	At School
☐ feed a pet	☐ take turns
☐ set the table	☐ get along with others
☐ clean my room	☐ follow rules
☐ tell the truth	☐ do my best work

It is your responsibility to cooperate with others. When you **cooperate,** you work together. You do not bully. You work well with others.

Got it?

4. Fact and Opinion **Read** the sentence below. **Write** whether it is a fact or an opinion.

You have the right to belong to a group.

_____

5. A classroom responsibility I have is to

my Story Ideas

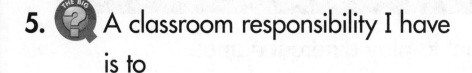

_____

_____

_____

□ **Stop!** I need help with _____

▶ **Go!** Now I know _____

Conflict and Cooperation

Cooperation means working with others. Conflict means not getting along. One way to end conflict is to show respect and cooperate.

The children want to play different games.

The children choose one game to play together.

1. **Look** at the picture. The children want to do different things.

2. **Draw** a picture to show how the children can work together to end conflict.

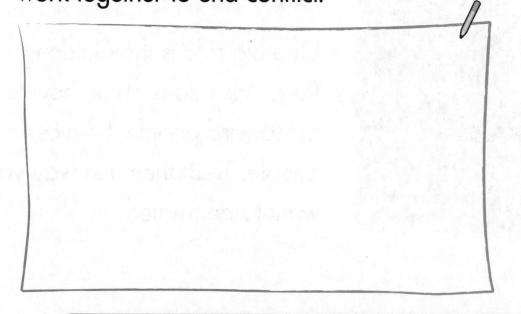

Lesson 3

I Follow Rules

 **Envision It!**

Circle the signs that show what people should or should not do.

You raise your hand if you want to say something in class. That is a class rule. Rules tell us what to do. Rules also tell us what not to do.

Rules keep us safe. They help us get along with others. They keep things fair.

One big rule is the Golden Rule. This rule is about how to act toward people. Be nice to people. Treat them the way you want to be treated.

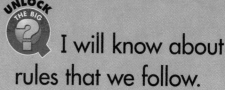
Rules at Home and School

We have rules at home. We have rules at school. We are nice to people. We take care of our things. We put things where they belong. We leave other people's things alone. We take turns.

Sometimes a group votes to make a rule. To **vote** is to make a choice. Each person has one vote. The choice with the most votes is what the group does.

1. ◉ **Fact and Opinion**
Underline one fact above about rules.

Laws in the Community

Communities have rules, too. A rule for a community is called a **law.** Laws tell us what we must do. They also tell us what we must not do.

One law is that children must go to school. It makes sure we have an education. Another law is to wear a helmet when you ride a bike. This law keeps us safe. Another law is to put trash where it should go. This law keeps our community clean.

2. **Fill in** the blank using the details above to help you.

_____

_____ help keep people safe.

3. ◉ **Compare and Contrast** What is one rule you follow both at home and at school?

_____

_____

_____

_____

4. **?** One rule I follow at school is   **my Story Ideas**

_____

_____

_____

_____

■ **Stop!** I need help with _____

_____

▶ **Go!** Now I know _____

My Leaders

Envision It!

Circle people who are in charge.

A **leader** helps people decide what to do. Leaders can make rules. They make sure we follow rules, too.

Leaders help us at home, at school, and in the community. One leader at school is the principal.

1. **Fill in** the blank using the details above to help you.

_____

The _____

makes rules for a school.

Leaders at Home

We have leaders at home. They can be mothers and fathers. They can be grandparents. Older brothers and sisters can be leaders, too.

Leaders at home keep you safe. They keep you healthy. They make rules so everyone gets along.

2. ◎ **Fact and Opinion Read** the sentences below. Circle the opinion.

A grandparent is a leader.

Grandparents are the best leaders.

Leaders at School

The principal and teachers are leaders at school. They help you follow rules. Other school leaders keep you safe. They make sure you follow rules on the bus and at lunch. Coaches make sure you play fair.

You can be a leader, too. One way is to do a classroom job. Another way is to be a team captain.

Leaders in the Community

Many community leaders want people to be safe. They make sure people follow laws. Police officers make sure people stop at red lights. Firefighters keep people safe from a fire. Doctors help sick people feel better.

3. Fill in the blank.

We have leaders at school and in the

_____

- -

_____

4. ⊙ **Main Idea and Details Read** the
sentences below. **Circle** the main idea.

A coach is a school leader. The coach teaches
children how to play sports.

5. ❓ A leader in my school helps us by   **my Story Ideas**

✏️ -

_____

⬛ **Stop!** I need help with _____

- -

▶️ **Go!** Now I know _____

Lesson 5
My Government

Envision It!

Circle the people who work for the community.

Think what might happen if no one was in charge. There would be no one to help make our laws. There would be no one to decide what communities need.

A **government** is made up of citizens. They are in charge. They work together to make rules and laws. They work so citizens have good places to live.

We have three kinds of government. We have government for our community, our state, and our country.

Government leaders meet at the Town Hall of Redington Shores, Florida.

UNLOCK THE BIG ? I will know how government helps us.

Vocabulary
government
mayor
governor
president

Community Government

The **mayor** is the leader in many communities. Other leaders work with the mayor in community government.

These leaders make rules and laws for the community. They make sure there are police and firefighters. They make sure trash is collected.

1. ◎ **Fact and Opinion**
   <u>Underline</u> facts above about what community leaders do.

Capitol building in
Tallahassee, Florida

President Barack Obama

State Government

The leader of a state is the **governor.** The governor works with other leaders in the state government.

These leaders make rules and laws for the state. They make sure the state has schools. They make sure roads are safe.

2. **Fill in** the blank using the details above to help you.

The _____

is the leader of a state.

National Government

The leader of our country is the **president.** Citizens vote to choose the president. The president works with leaders from around our nation. They make laws for all the people in our country.

The national government makes sure all people are treated fairly. It makes sure that mail gets to the right places. It keeps citizens safe.

3. **Underline** one thing the president does.

---

4. ◉ **Cause and Effect** How does our country choose a new president?

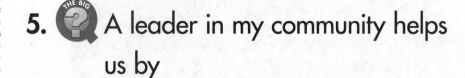

5. ❓ A leader in my community helps us by

my Story Ideas

⬜ **Stop!** I need help with _____

▶ **Go!** Now I know _____

Fact and Opinion

Some sentences give facts. A fact is true.

Some sentences give opinions. An opinion tells how someone feels. It often starts with the words "I think."

Fact   The White House is in Washington, D.C.

Opinion   I think the White House is the most beautiful building in Washington, D.C.

1. Look at the picture. **Read** the sentences below it.

I think firefighters have the most important job.

Firefighters work together to put out fires.

2. Underline the sentence that gives a fact.

3. Circle the sentence that gives an opinion.

Symbols of My Country

Envision It!

Circle the flag of our country.

Uncle Sam is a symbol of our country.

Our country is the United States of America. Our red, white, and blue flag is a symbol of our country. A **symbol** is something that stands for something else. Our country has many symbols.

1. ◎ **Fact and Opinion**
   Read the sentences below. Circle the opinion.

   The American flag is a symbol of our country.

   Red, white, and blue are the best flag colors.

American Symbols

The Statue of Liberty stands for hope and freedom. The Liberty Bell also stands for freedom. The White House stands for the government of our country. It is where the president lives. The bald eagle is a living symbol of our country. It stands for strength and freedom.

Statue of Liberty

2. **Fill in** the blank using the details above to help you.

The Liberty Bell and the bald eagle are _____ both symbols of _____ .

bald eagle

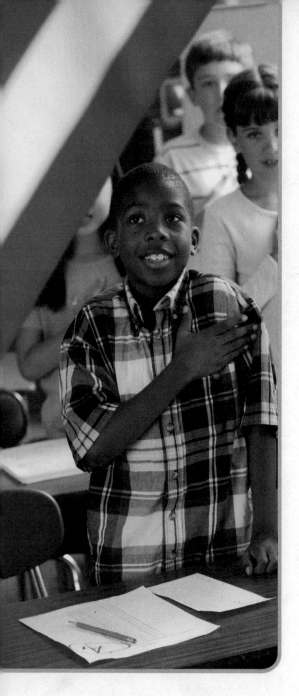

Songs and the Pledge of Allegiance

We sing songs to show we care about our country. "The Star-Spangled Banner" and "My Country, 'Tis of Thee" are both songs about our country. We also sing "America." We face the flag to say the Pledge of Allegiance. This shows we care about our country, too.

3. **Underline** the names of three American songs.

United States Papers

The Declaration of Independence is an important paper. Leaders who lived long ago wrote this paper. It helped to make our country free.

When our country was new, leaders made a plan for making laws. This plan is the Constitution.

The Constitution lists rights and freedoms of people in our country.

United States Constitution

4. **Underline** the names of two important papers.

5. ◉ **Fact and Opinion** **Read** the sentence below. **Write** whether it is a fact or an opinion.

The Statue of Liberty is an American symbol.

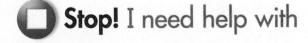

6. ❓ I am a good citizen in my community when

my Story Ideas

◻ **Stop!** I need help with

▷ **Go!** Now I know

Review and Assessment

Lesson 1

1. What is one responsibility of a good citizen in a community?

Lesson 2

2. Draw a picture of a responsibility you have at home or at school.

3. ⦿ **Fact and Opinion Read** the sentences below.
Underline the fact. ⟨**Circle**⟩ the opinion.

A. I think we need a law that puts bike lanes on every street.

B. A rule tells us what to do and what not to do.

Lesson 4

4. **Look** at the words in the box. **Write** the leaders in the correct places on the chart.

principal   grandfather   teacher   mother

Leaders	
Home	**School**
older sister	bus driver

Lesson 5

5. Underline the name of the leader of our country.

mayor   governor   president

Lesson 6

6. Fill in the bubble next to the correct answer.

Which of the following is a symbol of our president?

Ⓐ Statue of Liberty

Ⓑ Liberty Bell

Ⓒ White House

Ⓓ bald eagle

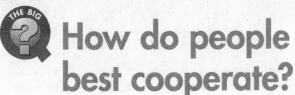

Go online to write and illustrate your own **myStory Book** using the **myStory Ideas** from this chapter.

How do people best cooperate?

In this chapter you learned about being a good citizen.

Draw a picture of people in your community who are being good citizens.

While you're online, check out the **myStory Current Events** area where you can create your own book on a topic that's in the news.

Work in the Community

How do people get what they need?

Draw a picture of yourself doing a job at school or at home.

my Story Video

 # Begin With a Song

Trucks and Buses

Sing to the tune of "On Top of Old Smokey."

Cindy's a plumber.
She unclogs the tub.
She unclogs the sink, too,
And gives it a scrub.

George drives a big truck
With his puppy in back.
George has all the lumber
In one giant stack.

Vocabulary Preview

needs

wants

choice

scarce

goods

Circle examples of these words in the picture.

services

producer

consumer

market

job

What We Need, What We Want

Envision It!

1 2

Look at the two scenes.

There are things people must have to live. There are things people like to have.

People Have Needs

Needs are things we must have to live. Food and water are needs. We must eat and drink to live. We also need clothing and shelter. **Shelter** is a place to live.

1. **Look** at the picture on this page. **Circle** things that show needs.

Write the number of the scene that matches the items.

Vocabulary

needs   wants
shelter   money

People Have Wants

Wants are things we would like to have. We do not need these things to live. A TV is a want. It is fun to watch. It is not something we need to live.

2. **Think** of a need and a want that are not shown in the chart. **Write** the need and want where they belong in the chart.

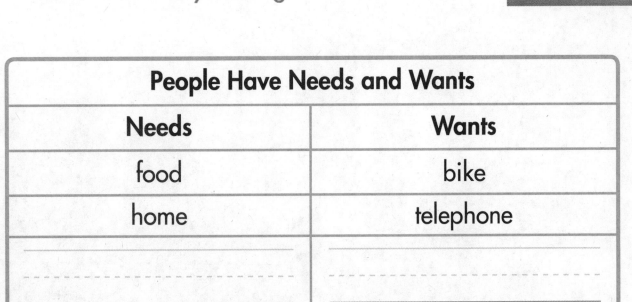

People Have Needs and Wants	
Needs	**Wants**
food	bike
home	telephone

Meeting Needs and Wants

All people have the same needs. They need food and water. They need clothing and shelter. People have different wants. They want toys, or cars, or other things.

People meet their needs in different ways. Some grow their own food. Others sew, or produce, their own clothing. Some build their own homes.

Most people use money to buy the things they need and want. **Money** is coins or bills that are used to buy things. People work to earn money.

3. **Cause and Effect Read** the sentences below. **Circle** the cause.

People need money to buy things.

People work to earn money.

Got it?

4. **Fact and Opinion Read** the sentence below. **Write** whether it is a fact or an opinion.

We all need food to live.

_____

_____

5. How do most people meet their needs?

my Story Ideas

_____

_____

_____

_____

⬛ **Stop!** I need help with _____

▶ **Go!** Now I know _____

Why We Make Choices

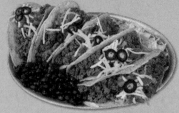

Envision It!

Which would you choose to eat?
Mark an X on your choice.

Sometimes we can not have all we want. Then we have to make a choice. We make a **choice** when we pick between two things. We pick one thing. We leave the other thing.

1. **Look** at the pictures. Which food do you think would be a good choice for dinner? Circle that food.

$2

$4

$7

_____

_____

_____

_____

Write why you chose it.

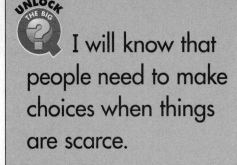
UNLOCK THE BIG ? I will know that people need to make choices when things are scarce.

Vocabulary
....
choice   trade-off
scarce

We Choose What to Buy

Sometimes there is not enough of something. When there is not enough of something, it is **scarce.** Look at the picture. Three children want to use the computer. There is only one computer. Computers in this class are scarce.

Money can be scarce, too. People may not have enough money for all they need and want. They must make choices about what to buy.

2. ⊙ **Cause and Effect**
   <u>Underline</u> the words above that tell why things can be scarce.

We Make Trade-Offs

Sometimes you have to make a choice between two things. You may want to play a game. You may want to watch a movie, too. You can not do them both at the same time. So, you have to make a choice. If you play the game, you do not watch the movie. When you make a choice, you make a trade-off. A **trade-off** is when you give up one thing to get something else. The thing you give up is called the opportunity cost.

3. Look at the pictures below. **Choose** the one you would like to do. **Circle** your choice.

4. ⊙ **Cause and Effect** Read the sentences below. **Underline** the effect.

Three children want apples for a snack. There is only one apple. Two children must pick a different snack.

5. (?) Think of a time you had to choose between two things. What did you choose? How did you decide?

my Story Ideas

■ **Stop!** I need help with _____

▶ **Go!** Now I know _____

Goods and Services

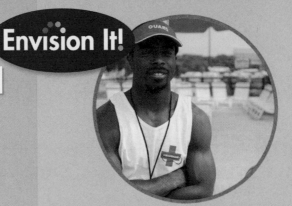

Mark an *X* on the people who make things.

Some workers do things for people. Other workers make things. People buy these things to meet their needs.

What Are Goods?

Goods are things people grow or make. People grow corn. They grow apples, too. Corn and apples are goods. People make bread. They make shirts, too. Bread and shirts are goods.

1. **Circle** the names of goods in the text above.

You can find goods at home, at school, and in the community. Toys and food are some goods you find at home. Desks and paper are some goods you find at school. Library books and cars are some goods you find in the community.

2. ◎ **Cause and Effect Read** the sentences below. **Underline** the effect.

Children like to play with toys and games.

The worker makes toys for children.

What Are Services?

Services are jobs people do to help others. Doctors and nurses help sick people. Helping sick people is a service. Fixing cars and mowing lawns are services, too.

Schools have service workers. Teachers help you learn. Bus drivers drive you to and from school. Coaches show you how to play sports.

Communities have service workers, too. Police and firefighters help keep you safe. Mail carriers bring mail to your home.

3. **Write** the name of a service worker in your community.

4. ⊙ **Compare and Contrast Write** two goods and two services in the chart.

Kinds of Goods and Services	
Goods	**Services**

5. ❓ What kind of service would you like to do for other people?

 my Story Ideas

■ Stop! I need help with _____

▶ Go! Now I know _____

Cause and Effect

Tina walked down the street. It started to rain. Tina opened her umbrella.

cause

effect

A cause is what makes something happen. What caused Tina to open her umbrella? It started to rain.

An effect is what happens. What effect did the rain have? Tina opened her umbrella.

Read the sentences. Then **look** at the pictures.

Travis made a tower with blocks. His dog ran into the tower. The tower fell.

1. What made the tower fall? **Write** the cause.

_____

_____

2. What happened to the tower? **Write** the effect.

_____

_____

Buying and Selling

Look at the boots.

People get goods and services in different ways. One way is to trade. When we **trade,** we give one thing to get something else. We can trade goods we make. We can trade services. We can also trade money for goods and services.

1. ◎ **Main Idea and Details**
   Circle the main idea in the text above.

HOME GROWN TOMATOES

FRESH Lemonade

Draw a picture of where you could go to buy the boots.

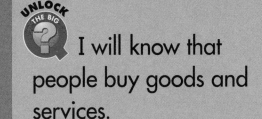
Producers and Consumers

A **producer** grows or makes goods. Bakers are producers. Bakers make bread. Producers may sell the goods they make.

A **consumer** uses goods and services. Consumers buy the bread that bakers make. Producers can be consumers, too. They buy things they need to make goods. Bakers buy flour to make bread.

2. Write what a producer does.

_____

- - - - - - - - - - - - - - - - - -

_____

Markets

Producers may take the goods they make to markets. A **market** is a place where goods are sold. Consumers buy things at markets. You can find food, clothes, toys, and other goods at markets.

3. **Circle** goods in the pictures.

Got it?

4. ⊙ **Main Idea and Details** **Read** the sentences. ⟨Circle⟩ the main idea.

Producers grow or make goods. Farmers are producers. They grow goods. Bakers are producers. They make goods.

5. ❓ Think of a job as a producer you would like to have. What would you produce?   my Story Ideas

_____

⬛ **Stop!** I need help with _____

▶ **Go!** Now I know _____

Spending and Saving

Mark an X on each picture that shows how money can be used.

Long ago, people traded goods and services. A person who mended chairs wanted eggs. A person with a lot of eggs had a broken chair. They traded their goods and services. Then they both got what they wanted.

1. **Look** at the picture of the children holding stickers.

   (Circle) the goods they are trading.

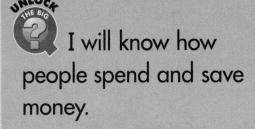
Using Money

People do not always have a good or service to trade. So today most people use money to trade. They trade money for goods. They trade money for services. People use money to buy what they need and want.

2. **Fill in** the blank using the details above to help you.

_____

People use money to _____
what they need and want.

Saving Money

People can spend money now or save it. To **save** money means to put it away until later. People save until they have enough money to buy what they need or want. Most people save money in a bank. Banks keep money safe.

Some people borrow money from a bank. To **borrow** means to take something and promise to return it. People borrow money to buy what they need or want now.

Bea wants a bike. She does not have enough money. So she works to earn money. She saves money for a long time. At last, she has enough money. She buys the bike she wants!

3. ◉ **Cause and Effect** (Circle) the reason Bea saves her money. **Underline** the effect.

Got it?

4. ⊙ **Fact and Opinion Read** the sentence below. **Write** whether it is a fact or an opinion.

I think it is better to trade with goods than to trade with money.

_____

5. ❓ If you do not have enough money for something, what do you do?

my Story Ideas

_____

_____

🔲 **Stop!** I need help with _____

▶ **Go!** Now I know _____

Charts and Graphs

A chart is a way to show things using words, numbers, and pictures. A title tells what the chart is about. Rows and columns show information.

Ashley has a job. She walks dogs to earn money. Look at the chart below. The left side lists the weeks Ashley worked. The right side lists how much money she earned.

row ▶

Money Earned From Walking Dogs	
Week	**Money earned**
Week 1	$2
Week 2	$5
Week 3	$3
Week 4	$2

▲ **column**

Try it!

1. **Look** at the chart on this page. The chart shows the money Ashley earned pulling weeds. **Circle** the title.

2. How much money did Ashley earn weeding in Week 2?

3. **Underline** the week when she earned $4.

4. **Underline** the money she earned in week 4.

Money Earned From Weeding	
Week	**Money earned**
Week 1	$3
Week 2	$2
Week 3	$4
Week 4	$3

Jobs People Do

Envision It!

Sue feeds the classroom fish. It is one way she helps at school.

People work at jobs. A **job** is the work people do. Working to produce hats is a job. Working at a store selling goods is a job.

Many people work at jobs to earn money. Some people work because they want to help others. They do not earn money for their jobs.

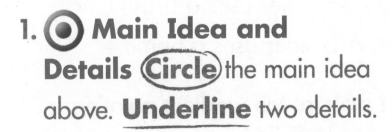

Draw a picture of one way you help at home or at school.

Jobs at Home

People do jobs at home to help their families. One job is to keep your room clean. Another job is to take care of a pet.

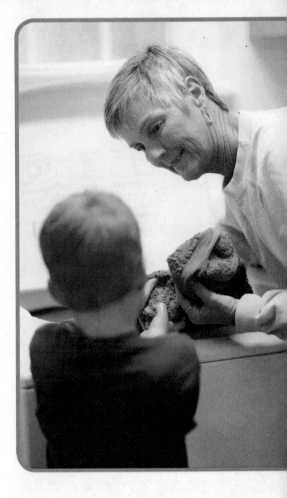

Some jobs people do at home earn money. People can make things to sell. Some people sew clothing. They sell the clothing to earn money.

1. ◉ **Main Idea and Details** Circle the main idea above. **Underline** two details.

Jobs at School

People have jobs at school. Teachers and principals help children learn. Cooks work to feed children. These workers produce services.

Children work at school, too. They listen. They ask questions. They learn.

2. Look at the picture. **Circle** the person doing a job at school.

Different Jobs

People work at different jobs. Many people are needed to do some jobs. It takes many people to make a car or build a house.

Some people use tools to do their jobs. A painter uses a brush as a tool. A builder uses a hammer.

3. Look at the workers painting a mural. **Circle** someone using a tool.

4. ⊙ **Cause and Effect Read** the sentences below.
   Ⓒⓘⓡⓒⓛⓔ the cause. **Underline** the effect.

   Most people work at jobs.
   They earn money for their work.

5. **?** What different jobs do people
   have in your community?

   my **Story Ideas**

   Stop! I need help with _____

   Go! Now I know _____

Lesson 1

1. **Write** *want* or *need* under each picture.

_____

_____

_____

_____

Lesson 2

2. <u>**Underline**</u> the choice that has an example of something that is scarce.

A. There is one glass of milk. Two children want milk.

B. There are two glasses of milk. Two children want milk.

3. Look at the words in the box. Decide if they are goods or services. **Write** the words where they belong in the chart.

books   teaching   driving   apples

Kinds of Goods and Services	
Goods	**Services**
beds	cleaning

4. Which picture shows a producer? **Circle** the producer.

Lesson 5

5. ⊙ **Cause and Effect Read** the sentences below. **Circle** the cause. **Underline** the effect.

Vijay wanted to buy a new basketball. He saved his money and bought the basketball.

Lesson 6

6. **Fill in** the bubble next to the correct answer.

Which is a job people do at school?

(A) fold clothes

(B) sell shoes

(C) cook food

(D) make the bed

Go online to write and illustrate your own **myStory Book** using the **myStory Ideas** from this chapter.

How do people get what they need?

In this chapter you have learned about how people work for what they need or want.

Draw a picture of a job you would like to do when you grow up.

While you're online, check out the **myStory Current Events** area where you can create your own book on a topic that's in the news.

Looking at Our World

What is the world like?

Think of a place where you like to play outdoors. **Draw** what you see there.

my Story Video

♫ Begin With a Song

Show You Care

by Emily Sasaki

Sing to the tune of "Yankee Doodle."

You may live upon the plains
Or near a hill or lake.
Show you care about the earth.
There are simple steps to take!

Care for land and wildlife, too.
Let's take care of our nation.
Keep our air and water clean
And practice conservation!

Vocabulary Preview

map

globe

mountain

desert

ocean

Where Animals Live

mountains

desert

lake

ZOO MAP

1. Ducks
2. Seals
3. Entrance
4. Birds

N
W E
S

lake

continent

reduce

reuse

recycle

STOP

55

Where Things Are Located

Envision It!

Circle the chair next to the teacher's desk.

Direction words tell where things are. A **direction** is a place to look or a way to go. *Left* and *right* are direction words. So are *in front of* and *behind*. In the picture the bus is in front of the school.

1. ◉ **Main Idea and Details Underline** a sentence that gives details about direction words.

HURSTON ELEMENTARY SCHOOL

BUS

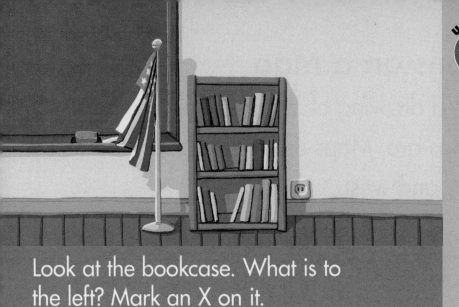

Look at the bookcase. What is to the left? Mark an X on it.

UNLOCK THE BIG ?

I will know that directions help us locate places and things.

Vocabulary

direction

map

Where Places Are

We can use direction words to say where places are. In the picture the fire house is to the left of the brown house. The word *left* tells us where to look.

2. **Draw** a tree to the right of the brown house.
   Draw yourself in front of the fire house.

Directions on a Map

A **map** is a drawing of a real place. It shows where things are. Maps use the directions north, south, east, and west.

Look at the map below. Put your finger on the school. Move your finger to the arrow marked West. The playground is west of the school.

3. Circle what is east of the playground on the map.

4. ⦿ **Main Idea and Details** **Read** the sentences below. (Circle) the main idea.

I can use direction words to say where my bike is. My bike is behind the house. It is under a tree.

5. ❓ **Think** of a place where you like to play. Use direction words. **Write** where it is.

my Story Ideas

_____

_____

_____

_____

⬛ **Stop!** I need help with _____

_____

▶ **Go!** Now I know _____

Envision It!

Look at the map. How can you get from the elephants to the lions?

Earth is where we live. It is round, like a ball. Earth is made up of land and water.

Globes

A **globe** is a round model of Earth. It shows all the land and water on Earth. The blue part on the globe shows water. The brown and green parts show land.

1. ◉ **Main Idea and Details** Circle the main idea in the text above.

Zoo

lions

Draw a line on the path to show how to get there.

Vocabulary

globe
key

Maps

Maps also show land and water, but maps are flat. Maps can show large places, like states. They can show small places, like towns.

A state map can show roads and the names of towns. A town map can show streets and buildings.

Some maps have a key. The **key** tells what the pictures on the map mean.

2. **Look** at the map.
   (Circle) the key.

North

Our Town

West   East

Key

🏦 bank   📜 pond

🏪 market   ⛪ school

South

Finding Places on a Map

We can use maps to find places. The map below shows all 50 states in our country. It also shows Washington, D.C. This is our nation's capital.

Look at the key. It shows a star for the national capital. Find the star on the map. The star marks where Washington, D.C. is.

3. Look at the map below.
    (Circle) the name of your state.

North

The United States of America

Washington
Oregon
Idaho
Montana
North Dakota
Minnesota
New Hampshire
Vermont
Maine
Nevada
Utah
Wyoming
South Dakota
Wisconsin
Michigan
New York
Massachusetts
Rhode Island
Connecticut
New Jersey
Delaware
Maryland
Washington, D.C.
California
Colorado
Nebraska
Iowa
Illinois
Indiana
Ohio
Pennsylvania
West Virginia
Virginia
Arizona
New Mexico
Kansas
Missouri
Kentucky
North Carolina
South Carolina
Oklahoma
Tennessee
Arkansas
Alabama
Georgia
Texas
Mississippi
Louisiana
Florida
Alaska
Hawaii

Key
⭐ national capital

West

East

South

4. ⊙ **Compare and Contrast** How are maps and globes alike? How are they different?

Alike _____

_____

_____

Different _____

_____

5. 🄰 Think about a map of your neighborhood. What is one thing you would put in the key?

my Story Ideas

_____

_____

_____

⬛ **Stop!** I need help with _____

▶ **Go!** Now I know _____

Parts of a Map

A map has many parts. The title tells what the map shows. The title of this map is Downtown. The compass rose shows directions. Arrows show N for north, S for south, E for east, and W for west. Map symbols are pictures that stand for real things. The key tells what the symbols mean. The library symbol on the map shows where the library is.

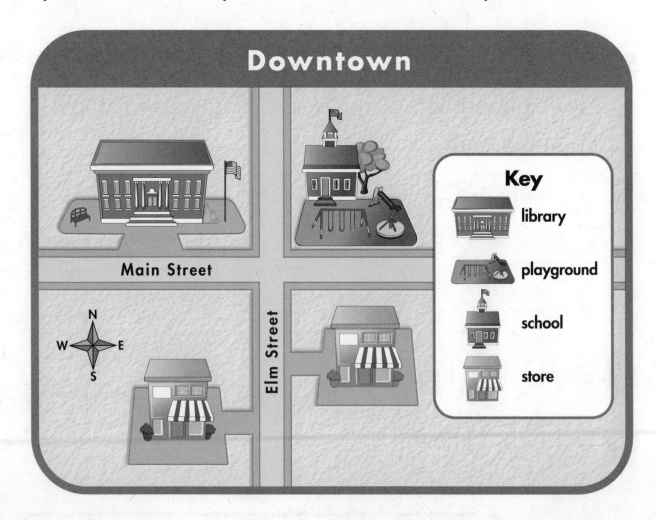

1. **Circle** the compass rose on the map below.

2. **Underline** the symbol for the fire house on the map and in the key.

3. **Draw** a map like the one below of your neighborhood. Show the places near your school.

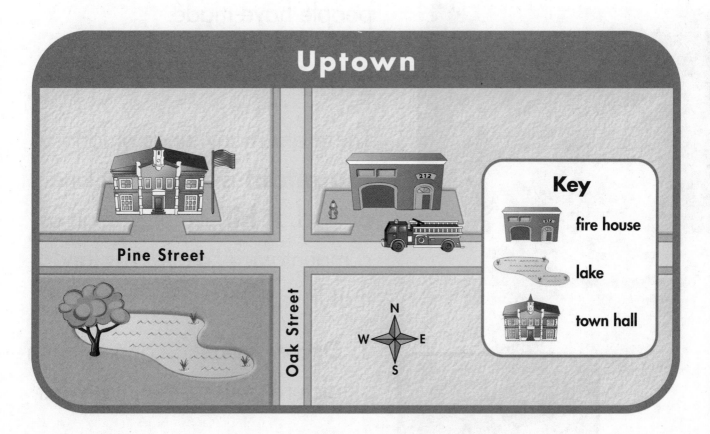

Envision It!

Color the land brown.
Color the water blue.

Earth is made up of land and water. Land and water are part of nature. Places on Earth have things from nature and things people have made.

Land

There are many kinds of land. A **mountain** is the highest kind of land. A **hill** is not as high as a mountain. A **desert** is land that is very dry.

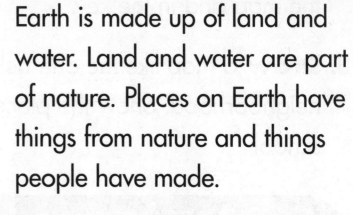

1. **Draw** a line to connect each picture to its name in the text.

UNLOCK THE BIG ?

I will know about different forms of land and water on Earth.

Vocabulary

mountain	ocean
hill	lake
desert	river

Water

There are different bodies of water. An **ocean** is a very large body of water. Ocean water is salty. A **lake** has land on all sides. Lakes are smaller than oceans. A **river** is long. Rivers flow toward a lake or an ocean. The water in most lakes and rivers is not salty.

2. **Draw** a line to connect each picture to its name in the text.

People Make Changes

People build things on Earth's land and water. They build bridges over water. They build houses on land. They build places to work and play. People often use things from nature to make these places.

3. ◉ **Main Idea and Details** What is the main idea in the text above? **Write** it on the lines below.

4. ⊙ **Compare and Contrast** **Write** one way lakes and oceans are alike. **Write** one way they are different.

✏ Alike

Different

5. ? What kind of land or water is near   my Story Ideas
your community?

✏

⏹ **Stop!** I need help with _____

▶ **Go!** Now I know _____

Lesson 4

Continents and Oceans

Envision It!

This is a picture of the United States. It is taken from space.

A map of the world can show all of Earth. The map below shows all of Earth's land and water. Most of Earth is covered by water.

The World

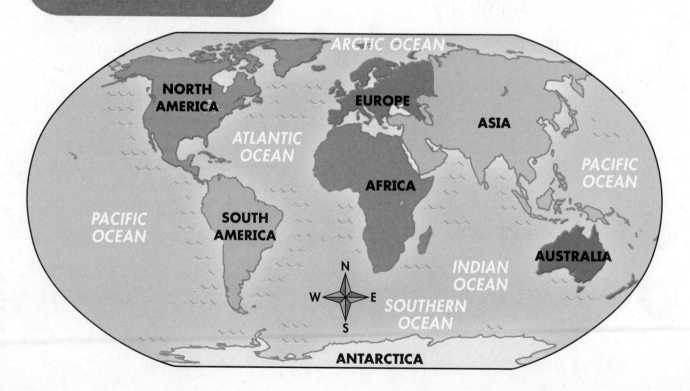

ARCTIC OCEAN

NORTH AMERICA

EUROPE

ASIA

ATLANTIC OCEAN

PACIFIC OCEAN

AFRICA

PACIFIC OCEAN

SOUTH AMERICA

AUSTRALIA

INDIAN OCEAN

N W E S

SOUTHERN OCEAN

ANTARCTICA

100

Write what the green and brown areas in the picture show.

Continents and Oceans

A **continent** is a large area of land. There are seven continents on Earth. We live on the continent of North America.

There are five oceans on Earth. North America touches three oceans. It touches the Atlantic Ocean on the east. It touches the Pacific Ocean on the west. It touches the Arctic Ocean to the north.

1. ◎ **Main Idea and Details**
   (Circle) the main idea above.

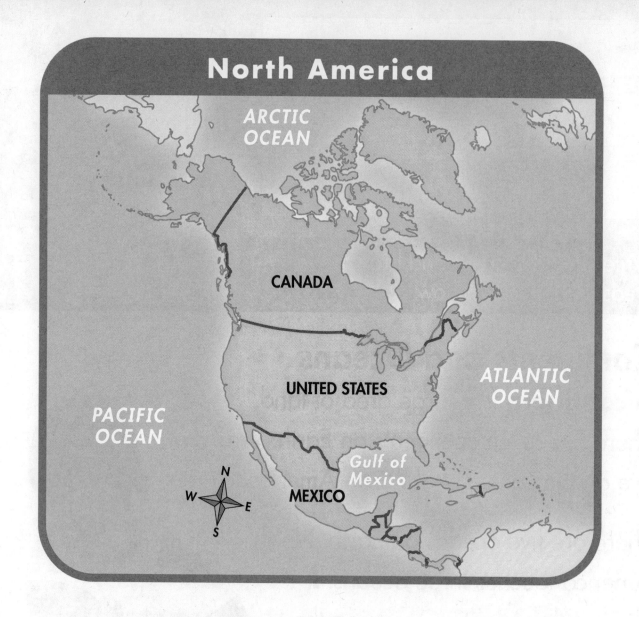

North America

The United States is a country on the continent of North America. Canada and Mexico are also countries in North America. Canada is north of the United States. Mexico is south of the United States.

2. Locate bodies of water on the map. **Circle** the Arctic Ocean, Pacific Ocean, and Atlantic Ocean. **Underline** the Gulf of Mexico.

Got it?

3. ◉ Main Idea and Details Read the sentences below. **Circle** the main idea. **Underline** the details.

Earth has many kinds of land and water. It has seven continents. It has five oceans.

4. On what continent is your community located?

Stop! I need help with _____

Go! Now I know _____

Lesson 5

Our Environment

Envision It!

Circle things that do not belong on a sunny beach.

Earth is our home. We use things on Earth to help us live.

Natural Resources

A resource is something we can use. Natural resources come from nature. We use water to drink, cook, and wash. We grow food in soil. We use trees to make things.

1. **Underline** three natural resources.

104

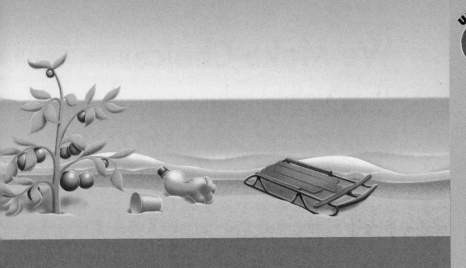

I will know how weather and natural resources affect the way we live.

Vocabulary

weather	reuse
reduce	recycle

Weather

Weather is what it is like outside at a certain time and place. Some places have hot weather. Some places have cold weather. Places can have dry, wet, or snowy weather.

Homes can keep us warm or cool. The weather helps us choose what kind of home to build.

2. Fill in the blank using the details above to help you.

Rain is a kind of

_____

- -

_____

We Make Choices

The weather helps us make other choices. It helps us choose clothes and things to do. We choose warm clothes when it is cold outside. We play some games when it is hot. We play other games when it is snowy.

3. ◉ **Main Idea and Details** (Circle) the main idea in the text above.

Caring for Earth

We can take care of our natural resources. When we **reduce,** we use less of something. When we **reuse,** we use something again. When we **recycle,** we take one thing and make it into something new.

4. **Underline** ways to care for Earth.

5. ⦿ **Cause and Effect** What kind of weather would cause you to wear a coat?

6. ? What natural resources are located near your community?

my Story Ideas

⬛ **Stop!** I need help with _____

▶ **Go!** Now I know _____

Main Idea and Details

Every story has a main idea. This is the most important, or big, idea. Details tell more about the main idea. The main idea of a paragraph is often the first sentence.

Look at the postcard below. David's family went to the lake. This is the main idea. They went swimming. They went out in a boat. These are details. They tell more about the main idea.

Dear Jeff,
My family took a trip to the lake. We had lots of fun. We went swimming. We went out in a boat.

David

Jeff Barrows
102 West Main Street
Dayton, Ohio 12345

1. **Read** the postcard from Jackie below.
2. **Circle** the main idea. **Underline** the details.

Dear Grandma,
We went to visit Aunt
Lexie in the mountains.
We rode sleds. We made
snowballs. It was cold,
but fun!

Jackie

Mrs. Mary Munoz
3002 West First Avenue
Tampa, FL 12345

Getting From Here to There

Circle the pictures that show ways you have used to go places.

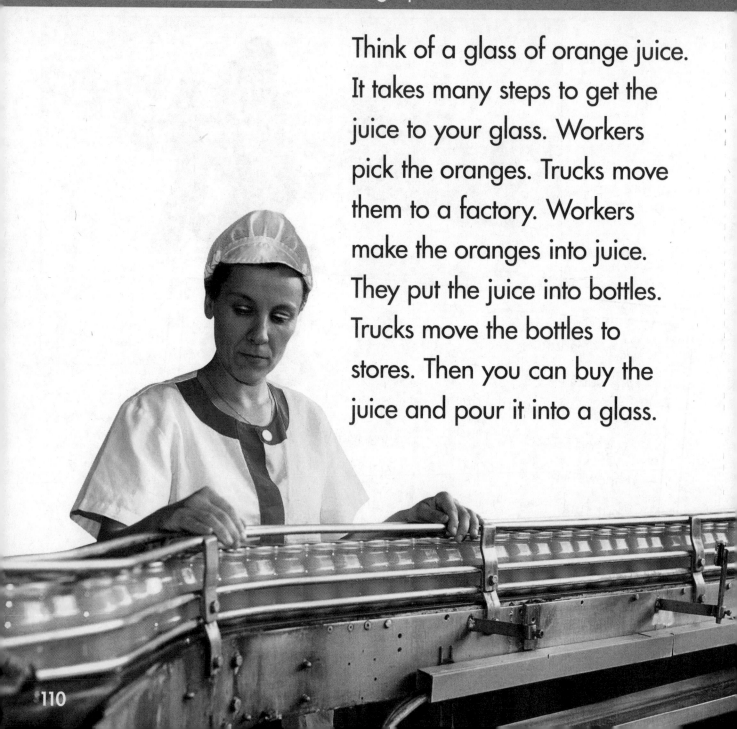

Think of a glass of orange juice. It takes many steps to get the juice to your glass. Workers pick the oranges. Trucks move them to a factory. Workers make the oranges into juice. They put the juice into bottles. Trucks move the bottles to stores. Then you can buy the juice and pour it into a glass.

UNLOCK THE BIG ?

I will know ways people in different places are connected.

Vocabulary
....
transportation
communicate

Transportation

Transportation is the way goods and people move from place to place. Trucks, airplanes, and ships are kinds of transportation. Trains, buses, and bikes are kinds of transportation, too.

We use transportation to go places. Sellers use it to move goods to stores. Buyers use it to go to stores to buy goods like orange juice.

1. **Write** words to finish the sentence.

I use transportation when I go to

_____

_____

Communication

You can communicate with people who live far away. To **communicate** is to give and get information. You can write a letter. You can use the telephone. You can use your computer to send a note.

2. ◎ **Main Idea and Details** (Circle) the main idea in the paragraph above. **Underline** three detail sentences.

3.  **Compare and Contrast Write** the words from the box where they belong on the chart.

| truck | telephone | computer | bus |

Transportation and Communication	
Transportation	**Communication**
_____	_____
_____	_____
_____	_____
_____	_____
_____	_____

4.  What types of transportation do you use in your community?

my Story Ideas

_____

_____

_____

_____

_____

⬛ **Stop!** I need help with _____

_____

▶ **Go!** Now I know _____

Lesson 1

1. Look at the map below. (Circle) the words that tell directions.

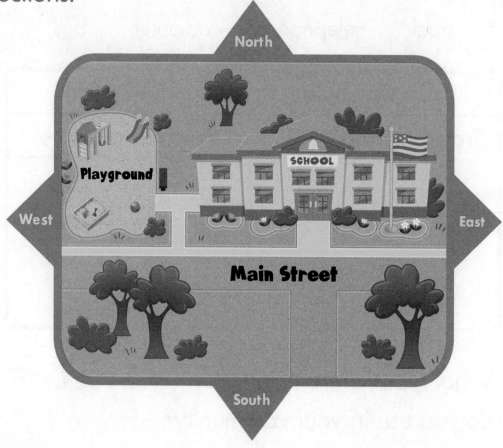

Lesson 2

2. Fill in the circle for the correct answer.

What does the key on a map show?

    Ⓐ title   Ⓒ globe

    Ⓑ symbols   Ⓓ directions

Lesson 3

3. **Write** N on the map to show something from nature. **Write** P on something made by people.

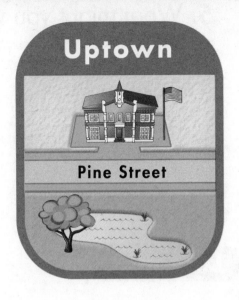

Uptown

Pine Street

Lesson 4

4. North America is on the top left. Florida points into the ocean on the east. **Mark** an X on the ocean name.

The World

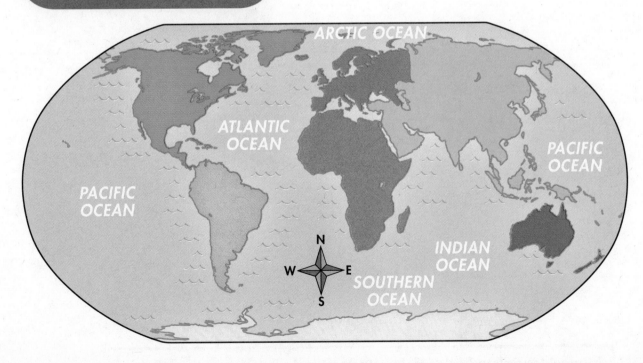

ARCTIC OCEAN

ATLANTIC OCEAN

PACIFIC OCEAN

PACIFIC OCEAN

INDIAN OCEAN

SOUTHERN OCEAN

N W E S

5. What might you wear if the weather is rainy?

6. ◉ **Main Idea and Details Read** the sentences below. (Circle) the main idea. **Write** one detail sentence.

There are many kinds of transportation. Trucks are often used to move goods. Buses are often used to move people.

Go online to write and illustrate your own **myStory Book** using the **myStory Ideas** from this chapter.

What is the world like?

Draw a map of a place you know well, such as your neighborhood.

While you're online, check out the **myStory Current Events** area where you can create your own book on a topic that's in the news.

Traditions We Share

How is culture shared?

Draw a picture of you and your family.
Show a favorite activity you do together.

my Story Video

🎵 Begin With a Song
Explore With Me!

Sing to the tune of "Hush, Little Baby."

Travel the world. Explore with me.
There are so many things to do and see.
There are people we will meet.
There are new foods we will eat.

We'll take a boat, a bus, and a train.
We'll fly around the world in a great
   big plane.
We'll learn many things we want to know.
We'll tell all about each place we go.

Vocabulary Preview

culture

celebrate

custom

hero

shelter

Circle examples of these words in the picture.

TACOS

LUIGI'S ITALIAN RESTAURANT

tradition

president

holiday

family

language

What Is Culture?

Envision It!

What is the same about these pictures? **Write** about it.

We all need food, clothes, and **shelter,** or a home. These things are also part of every culture. **Culture** is the way a group of people live. There are many different cultures. They have their own music, dance, art, religion, and language. **Language** is the words we speak.

What We Eat

Each culture has its own kinds of food. In our country, we can eat food from many cultures.

1. **Circle** foods you have tried.

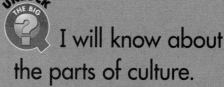

What We Wear

Clothing is a part of every culture. Our clothes are different. They are alike, too. We have clothes for school, work, and play. We have clothes for special days.

Clothing also shows where people in a culture live. In hot places, people wear clothes that keep them cool. In cold places, they wear clothes that keep them warm.

2. ◉ **Main Idea and Details**
   Circle a main idea above.
   Underline two details.

Where We Live

Homes also show where people in a culture live. In hot places, homes are made to keep heat out. In cold places, homes are made to keep heat in.

Homes are made from different things. Some homes are made of stone, mud, or brick. Other homes are made of wood from trees.

Some homes are made for one family. Other homes are made for many families.

3. **Look** at the pictures.
   Write one way these homes are different.

_____

_____

_____

_____

4. ◉ **Compare and Contrast** What is the same about all cultures? What is different?

5. ? What is one thing you would like to tell someone about your culture?   my Story Ideas

⬜ **Stop!** I need help with _____

▶ **Go!** Now I know _____

Families Are Alike and Different

Envision It!

Here are two different families.

A **family** is a group of people who live together. A family may be small. A family may be large.

All families are the same in some ways. The people in a family share the same culture. They take care of each other. They each have responsibilities in their family.

Family Customs

Families have many customs. A **custom** is the way people usually do something.

Draw a picture of your family.

Vocabulary
family
custom

Some families sing together. Some families take long walks together. Other families make and eat special foods. These things are all customs.

The different customs families have make each family special. Yet each family has customs they share with other people.

1. **Circle** a custom shown in this picture.

Families Share Culture

Families share their culture with other people who live around them. The songs, dances, and foods that families share are part of a bigger community.

Look at the picture. A family owns this market. Here, they sell foods from their culture. When people buy and eat these foods, they share the family's culture.

2. ◉ **Compare and Contrast** How is this market like one in your community? How is it different?

_____

_____

_____

_____

_____

3. ◉ **Sequence Write** one sentence about a food custom you share with your family. **Tell** what you do first.

First, we _____

_____

_____

4. ❓ How do you share a meal with your family?

my Story Ideas

_____

_____

_____

_____

□ **Stop!** I need help with _____

▶ **Go!** Now I know _____

What Are Our Celebrations?

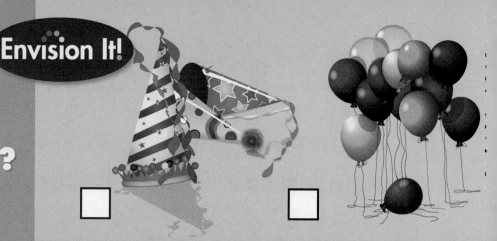

Envision It!

☐ ☐

Check a box to show each thing you use to celebrate.

Families have many traditions. A **tradition** is a way to do something that people pass down over time.

Families Celebrate

A wedding is a tradition. Many families **celebrate,** or do something special, at a wedding. Families celebrate reunions, too. Families who live far away from each other meet at a reunion. Families celebrate when a child finishes school, too.

1. ◎ **Main Idea and Details**
   Ⓒircle the main idea on this page. **Underline** one detail.

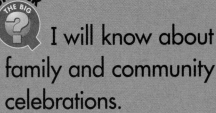
Vocabulary
....

tradition
celebrate
holiday

How We Celebrate

Many families celebrate holidays. A **holiday** is a special day. Some holidays honor people. Other holidays are religious traditions. Christmas, Passover, Eid al-Fitr, and Kwanzaa are some holidays.

How do families celebrate holidays? They may eat special foods. They may light candles. They may decorate their homes or give gifts.

2. **Write** the name of a holiday your family celebrates.

_____

_____

_____

Community Celebrations

Many communities celebrate their cultures. Some communities have parades. People play music. They dance. They eat special foods.

In some celebrations, people tell stories. Some stories are about important people. Others are about famous events from the past. Many people come to hear the stories. Children may help to tell the stories. Telling stories is a tradition in many communities.

3. Circle the person telling a story in this picture.

4. ◉ **Compare and Contrast** **Write** one way many holidays are alike. **Write** one way they are different.

Alike: ✎ _____
_____

Different: ✎ _____
_____

5. ❓ What is a community celebration where you live?

my **Story Ideas**

✎ _____
_____
_____
_____
_____

⬛ **Stop!** I need help with _____
_____

▶ **Go!** Now I know _____

Compare and Contrast

We compare to show how things are alike or the same. We contrast to show how things are different or not the same.

Look at the pictures on this page. Then read about where Jin and Matt live. How are their homes alike? How are they different?

Jin's home is made of wood. It has five rooms. One family lives here.

Matt's home is made of brick. It has five rooms. Many families live here.

Alike   Each home has five rooms.

Different   Jin's home is made for one family.
Matt's home is made for many families.

Jin goes to school. She wears a uniform. Jin likes to learn about science.

Matt goes to school. He wears jeans and a shirt. Matt likes to learn about math.

1. **Write** one way that Jin and Matt are alike.

_____

2. **Write** one way that Jin and Matt are different.

_____

_____

_____

We Celebrate Our Nation

Envision It!

(Circle) things in the picture that show a celebration.

A **hero** is someone who works hard to help others. We remember heroes on some holidays. We remember special events on holidays, too.

Our Nation's Heroes

Martin Luther King, Jr. is one of our heroes. We remember him on a holiday in January. King wanted all Americans to have the same rights. He worked to make the laws of our nation fair for everyone. A **nation** is a group of people who have one government.

UNLOCK THE BIG ?

I will know that we celebrate people and events from our nation's past.

Vocabulary

hero   president
nation   colony

George Washington was a hero, too. He helped our nation become free from Great Britain. Washington was the first **president,** or leader of our country. We remember him on Presidents' Day in February.

Veterans are men and women who fought for our country. We honor these brave people on Veterans Day in November.

1. Circle one of the heroes you read about. **Underline** a fact about this hero.

Our Nation's Holidays

We celebrate our nation's past on holidays. Thanksgiving is one holiday. July 4 is another.

Long ago, people came to this land from Great Britain to start colonies. A **colony** is land ruled by another country.

Many people in the colonies did not want to be ruled by another country. Leaders voted on a Declaration of Independence on July 4, 1776. It said the colonies wanted to be free. Now we celebrate Independence Day on July 4.

Independence Day celebration at the Statue of Liberty

2. ⊙ **Fact and Opinion** **Write** the letter *F* next to the fact. **Write** the letter *O* next to the opinion.

The colonies became independent. _____

The colony leaders were brave. _____

3. ⊙ **Cause and Effect** **Read** the sentences below. Circle the cause. **Underline** the effect.
People in the colonies wanted to be free.
They wrote a Declaration of Independence.

4. ? How do you celebrate one of our national holidays?

my Story Ideas

_____

_____

_____

_____

⬛ **Stop!** I need help with _____

▶ **Go!** Now I know _____

Stories From the Past

Envision It!

The pictures show the story of Johnny Appleseed.

Many stories tell about our country's past. Some stories tell facts about real people and events. A **fact** is something that is true. Annie Oakley and Davy Crockett were real people. Paul Bunyan and John Henry were not real people. Their stories are **fiction,** or made up.

Annie Oakley

Annie Oakley learned to hunt for food when she was young. She was very good at hunting. Later, Annie was part of Buffalo Bill's Wild West Show. There, she showed her hunting skills.

1. **Underline** a fact about Annie.

Draw what you think Johnny will do next.

UNLOCK THE BIG ? I will know the difference between historical fact and fiction.

Vocabulary

fact
fiction

Davy Crockett

Davy Crockett was born in Tennessee. As a boy, he farmed and drove a wagon. When he grew up, he was in the army.

Like Annie Oakley, Davy was good at hunting. He was a great bear hunter.

While in the army, Davy fought for Texas. Texas wanted to be free from Mexico. Davy died in the fight to free Texas. We tell stories about him today.

2. ◉ **Compare and Contrast** <u>Underline</u> words that tell how Davy Crockett was like Annie Oakley.

Paul Bunyan

Paul Bunyan was not a real person. The stories told about him are fiction. Paul grew to be very big. He used wagon wheels as buttons on his shirt!

Paul had a blue ox named Babe. Babe was as big and strong as Paul. Paul cut down trees and Babe took them away. Their footprints made big holes. The holes filled with rain and became lakes!

3. **Underline** a made-up detail.

John Henry

The story of John Henry is fiction. John Henry helped build the railroad. He used hammers to drill spikes into rocks. He did this faster than anyone else.

One day, railroad tracks had to go through a mountain. People thought a steam drill would be faster than John Henry. John Henry knew he was faster. He knew he could do the job.

Pound, pound, pound went John's hammers. He beat the steam drill!

4. **Underline** a made-up detail.

5. ◉ **Main Idea and Details Write** a detail that shows Paul Bunyan was not a real person.

6. **Which person from the lesson would you celebrate? Tell why.**

⬛ **Stop!** I need help with _____

▶ **Go!** Now I know _____

Lesson 6

Sharing Our Cultures

Envision It!

Look at the children playing their favorite game.

Children from other countries speak different languages. They have different cultures. Come meet some children from other countries.

Meet Choon-Hee

Hello! I am Choon-Hee from South Korea. When I get home from school, I leave my shoes by my front door. This is an old custom in my country. Next, I play music. Last, I set the table. We use chopsticks when we eat.

1. ⊙ **Sequence Write** 1, 2, or 3 by the sentence that tells what Choon-Hee does first, next, and last.

144

Draw a game that you like to play.

UNLOCK THE BIG ?

I will know that children from other countries have different cultures.

Vocabulary

fiesta

Meet Pedro

Hello! My name is Pedro. I live with my family in Mexico. My home is by the ocean. I like to swim. I like to play football. You call it soccer.

On Saturday, there will be a **fiesta,** or holiday, in my town. We will hear music. We will eat good food. We will play games and have fun.

2. **Write** one thing Pedro does that you would like to do.

Meet Hawa

I am Hawa from Mali. I live with my family. My mother is a teacher. One day, I want to be a teacher.

My family gets up at 7 o'clock. We eat breakfast. Then I walk to school. It takes 20 minutes to get there.

My class meets on the playground. We raise our country's flag. We sing our country's song.

3. **Underline** something that you and Hawa both do at school.

Meet Kurt

Guten Tag (GOO tun tahg)! That means "hello" in German. I live in a big city in Germany. I have a computer that I use at school. I also use it to write to friends far away.

4. **Circle** the words that mean "hello" in German.

146

5. ◉ **Compare and Contrast Write** one way you and the children in this lesson are alike. **Write** one way you are different.

6. What is your favorite thing from another culture? Where is it from?

my Story Ideas

■ **Stop!** I need help with _____

▶ **Go!** Now I know _____

Media and Technology

Using Graphic Sources

Graphic sources are photographs, charts, or pictures. You can use them to get information. Look at the picture. Ask questions about what you see. Then try to find answers in the picture.

Look at this photograph. Where is this place? What kind of place is it? How do people there get from place to place? The photograph shows a city in China. Many people ride bicycles. Some people walk. Others drive cars.

Look at the photograph below. **Write** what you see.

1. What kind of place is this?

2. How do people get from place to place?

Lesson 1

1. Draw something the people of a culture in a cold place might wear.

Lesson 2

2. ● Compare and Contrast Write one way families are the same. **Write** one way families are different.

Same: _____

_____

_____

Different: _____

_____

Lesson 3

3. **Circle** two celebrations.

Lesson 4

4. **Write** the name of a national hero. **Write** why we honor this person.

_____

_____

_____

_____

5. **Draw** a line to match each holiday with a picture.

Independence Day   Veterans Day

6. Fill in the bubble next to the correct answer.

The story about Annie Oakley is

   Ⓐ a true story.   Ⓒ about Buffalo Bill.

   Ⓑ a fictional story.   Ⓓ about a hunt for food.

Lesson 6

7. Draw lines to match a culture word with a photograph.

   celebration   music   language

 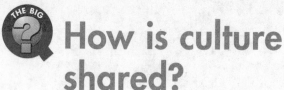
Go online to write and illustrate your own **myStory Book** using the **myStory Ideas** from this chapter.

? How is culture shared?

In this chapter, you learned about people and cultures from many places.

Think about your own culture.

Draw a family custom. **Label** your drawing.

While you're online, check out the **myStory Current Events** area where you can create your own book on a topic that's in the news.

Our Past, Our Present

THE BIG ? How does life change throughout history?

Draw a picture of what you would see if you could travel to the past.

my Story Video

 Begin With a Song

All Across the Country

Sing to the tune of "Skip to My Lou."

Long ago, we chopped down trees.

Built our houses, 1, 2, 3,

Life was simple all around me,

All across the country.

People in the kitchen, do, re, mi

Cakes on the table, 1, 2, 3

Sit on the benches, sit with me

All across the country.

Vocabulary Preview

clock

calendar

past

present

future

history

Circle examples of these words in the picture.

document

explorer

electricity

invention

communicate

transportation

157

Lesson 1
Measuring Time

Envision It!

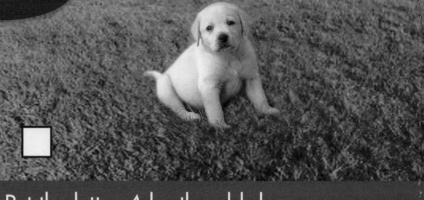

Put the letter A by the old dog.
Put the letter B by the young dog.

day

night

We **measure** time, or divide it up, in many ways. We talk about day and night. You go to school during the day. It is light outside. You go to bed at night. At night, it is dark outside.

We also measure time in days and weeks. There are 7 days in one week. You go to school from Monday to Friday. You are at home on Saturday and Sunday.

We measure time in months and years, too. There are 12 months in one year.

UNLOCK THE BIG ? I will know that we use clocks and calendars to measure time.

Vocabulary

measure
clock
calendar

Clocks Measure Time

Clocks help us measure time. A **clock** shows seconds, minutes, and hours. We use clocks to know the time of day or night.

Some clocks have hands. One hand points to the hours. One hand points to the minutes. Some clocks also have a hand that shows seconds. Other clocks show the time using numbers.

1. **Underline** words on these two pages that have to do with time.

Calendars Measure Time

A **calendar** is a chart. It shows the days, weeks, and months of the year. The name of the month is at the top of a calendar. Each box is one day.

A calendar helps us know about special days. Some boxes have pictures or words that show special days.

2. ⊙ **Sequence** (Circle) the first day of the month on this calendar.

MAY

Sunday	Monday	Tuesday	Wednesday	Thursday	Friday	Saturday
1	2	3	4	5	6	7
8 Mother's Day	9	10	11 Eric's Birthday	12	13	14
15	16	17	18	19	20	21
22	23	24	25	26	27	28
29	30 Memorial Day	31				

3. ◉ **Compare and Contrast** **Write** how clocks and calendars are the same. **Write** how they are different.

_____
_____
_____
_____

4. 🄱 What is your favorite month of the year? Why? **Write** about it.

my Story Ideas

_____
_____
_____
_____

◻ **Stop!** I need help with _____

▶ **Go!** Now I know _____

Reading Skills

Sequence

Sequence is the order in which things happen. We use clue words to tell about order. Some clue words are *first*, *next*, and *last*.

Look at the pictures. Then read the sentences below. See how the sentences match the pictures.

Keisha was busy at school.

First, she read a book.

Next, she learned about magnets.

Last, she played a game.

First   **Next**   **Last**

1. **Read** the paragraph below about what Carlos did on Saturday. **Underline** words that tell what happened first, next, and last.

   Carlos had fun on Saturday. First, he rode his bike. Next, he sorted his sports cards. Last, he played with his cat.

2. **Label** the pictures *first*, *next*, and *last*.

_____ _____ _____

_____ _____ _____

Talking About Time

Envision It!

Look at the pictures of the cars.
Label each one Old or New.

The **present** is what happens today. *Now* tells about the present.

The **past** is what happened before today. *Then* can tell about the past.

The **future** is what will happen after today. *Tomorrow* tells about the future.

People and places change over time. The girl in the picture has changed over time. In the past, she was 4 years old. She was shorter then. She is taller now.

1. **Underline** words that tell about time.

UNLOCK THE BIG ?

I will know how to describe events using the words *past, present,* and *future.*

Vocabulary
....

present   future
past   history

School Then and Now

Schools in the past were not like schools today. Children of all ages sat in the same classroom. Some children did not go to school.

Many more children go to school today. Children of the same age have their own classrooms. There are new tools to help children learn today.

2. **⊙ Compare and Contrast**

(Circle) things in the picture that have changed from the past to the present.

Communities Then and Now

Communities change over time. Today, there are more cars, homes, and people. Buildings today are taller than in the past.

Look at these pictures. One picture shows a community in the past. The other picture shows the same community today.

3. **Circle** one thing in the pictures that has changed from the past to the present.

History tells the story of people and places from the past. History also tells about events that happened long ago. Some communities have parades that celebrate their history.

4. ◎ **Compare and Contrast Write** how you have changed over time.

Last year, I

Now, I

5. **?** Would you travel in time to the past or to the future? Why?

my Story Ideas

◻ **Stop!** I need help with

▶ **Go!** Now I know

Timelines

A timeline shows the order of events. You read a timeline from left to right. The earliest event is on the left. The latest event is on the right. The timeline below shows four events in Anila's life.

What happened in 2011? First, find that year on the timeline. Put your finger on that year. Then look at the picture and words below 2011. Anila learned to write in 2011.

A Timeline of Anila's Life

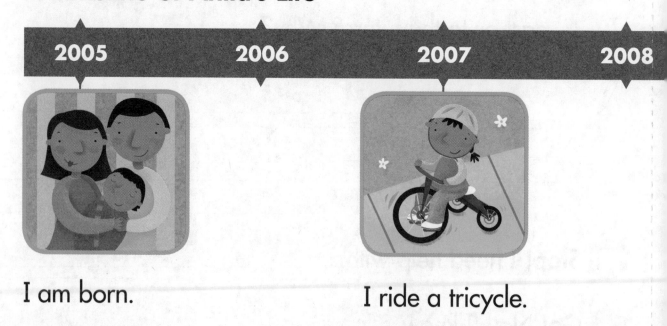

| 2005 | 2006 | 2007 | 2008 |

I am born.

I ride a tricycle.

Try it!

1. What could Anila do in 2007?

_____

2. **Circle** the earliest event shown on the timeline.

3. **Create** your own timeline like Anila's. Show important events.

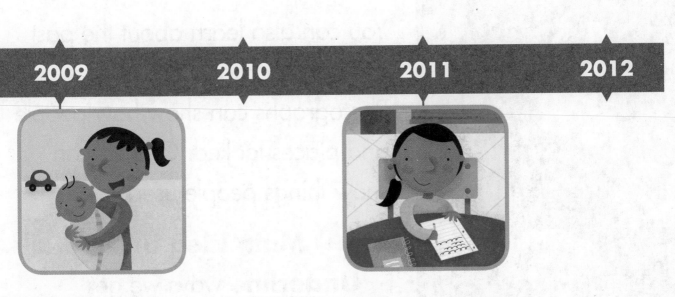

2009   2010   2011   2012

My brother is born.   I learn to write.

How We Learn About History

Photographs can show us about life in the past.

There are many ways to learn about history. You can listen to people tell stories about the past.

You can learn about history from documents. A **document** is a piece of paper with words on it.

You can also learn about the past from photographs and objects. Photographs can show how people and places looked. Objects can show things people used.

1. ◉ **Main Idea and Details**
   Underline ways we get information about the past.

Draw what you learned about your past from an old photograph.

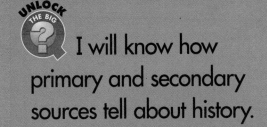
I will know how primary and secondary sources tell about history.

Vocabulary

document
primary source
secondary source

Primary Sources

Documents and photographs are primary sources. They tell us about people, places, and events of the past. A **primary source** is written or made by a person who was at an event.

A map can be a primary source. It can show what a place looked like in the past. A letter can also be a primary source. We can read it to learn about the past.

2. **Circle** the date that shows when this letter was written.

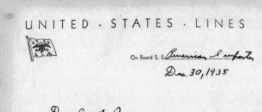

UNITED · STATES · LINES

On Board S. S. *American Importer*
Dec. 30, 1935

Dear Senator Moore:

I believe it will interest you to know how highly we have come to regard the officers and personnel of the New Jersey State Police since you appointed them to assist us in 1932. During this time I have learned to have the utmost confidence and respect for Col. Schwarzkopf and his organization. I feel that their work has always been

Secondary Sources

A **secondary source** also tells about people, places, and events from the past. These sources were written or made after the event happened. Your schoolbooks and books in the library are secondary sources.

3. **Underline** a secondary source.

Using Sources

How can you know if what a source says is true? You can ask questions about the source. Where did the information come from? Who wrote the source? When was the source made? Why was the source made?

You can also read many sources. Then you can see if the facts are the same. Good sources give the same facts.

4. **Underline** two ways you can tell if what a source says is true.

5. ⊙ **Compare and Contrast** **Fill in** the chart to show how a photograph and a letter about a past event are different.

	Photograph	Letter
Same	primary source	primary source
Different		

6. 🄱 You want to travel to a time in the past. How could you learn more about that time before you go?

⬜ **Stop!** I need help with _____

▶ **Go!** Now I know _____

American Heroes

Envision It!

Some coins show important people from the past.

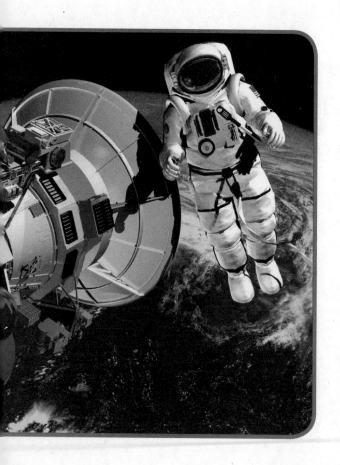

Heroes are people who work hard to help others. They are honest. People trust them. They face danger and must have courage. They take charge. They are responsible.

Heroes Explore

An **explorer** is a person who travels to learn about new places. Explorers go to places few people ever see. They go to new lands. They go under the ocean. They even go into space!

Draw your own coin that shows an important person.

UNLOCK
THE BIG

I will know about people who helped our country in the past.

Vocabulary

explorer

Long ago, people did not know how large our country was. Meriwether Lewis and William Clark went to find out. They were explorers. Lewis and Clark came back to tell others what they had seen.

They asked a Native American woman, Sacagawea (sak uh juh WEE uh), to help them. They met other Native Americans on their trip who did not speak English. Sacagawea helped them all talk to each other.

1. **Underline** the names of two explorers.

Thomas Jefferson

Abraham Lincoln

Harriet Tubman

Heroes Take Charge

There are many heroes in our country's history. Thomas Jefferson wrote the Declaration of Independence. This document said that our country should be free. Thomas Jefferson later became one of our presidents.

Abraham Lincoln was president during a war in our country. At that time, many African Americans were not free. Lincoln helped them to be free.

Harriet Tubman was an African American. She ran away to be free. Then she helped more than 300 other people to be free.

2. ◉ **Compare and Contrast Underline** a word that tells how Jefferson and Lincoln were alike.

3. **⊙ Cause and Effect** Choose one of the people you read about. How did this hero change people's lives?

_____

_____

_____

4. **❓** Which hero from the past would you want to meet? Why?   **my Story Ideas**

_____

_____

_____

☐ **Stop!** I need help with _____

▶ **Go!** Now I know _____

Envision It!

Which bike is from the past? Which bike is from the present?

Long ago, people used oil lamps for light. People did not have electricity. **Electricity** is a kind of energy. Today, lamps use electricity.

Electricity was an important invention. An **invention** is something that is made for the very first time.

Inventions can change the way we do things. Long ago, people washed clothes by hand. Today, we use a washing machine that runs on electricity. This invention makes life easier.

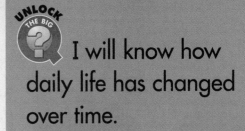

I will know how daily life has changed over time.

Vocabulary
electricity
invention

Write Past or Present by each bike.

Daily Life Then and Now

People need food, clothing, and shelter. Long ago, many people grew their own food. People made their own clothing. They built homes for their families.

Today, we get the things we need in different ways. Most people buy food and clothing in stores. We live in homes other people build.

1. **Main Idea and Details**
Circle the main idea above.
Underline the details.

School, Work, and Play

Some children went to school long ago. Others learned at home.

Most children did chores. They found wood for heat and cooking. They went out to get water. After chores, children played with toys. They also played games.

2. **Underline** chores children did long ago.

Families Then and Now

Every family has a history. You can look at photographs to learn about your family's past. Ask your family about their life in the past. Ask about school, work, and play.

3. **Write** one way you can learn about your family history.

4. ◉ **Compare and Contrast Complete** the chart. **Write** how life has changed from the past to the present.

Past	Present
oil lamp	*electricity*
made clothing	
grew food	

5. ❓ What one thing do you think has changed the most from the past to the present?

my Story Ideas

⬛ **Stop!** I need help with _____

▶ **Go!** Now I know _____

Technology Then and Now

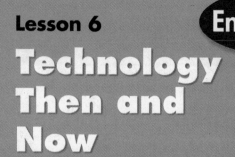

Envision It!

Circle ways you stay in touch with friends.

How can you talk to friends who live far away? You can call them. You can ride on a bus to visit them. Long ago, you could not do these things.

Communication Then

We **communicate** when we share information with others. Long ago, people had no telephones. They sent each other letters. This was a slow way to communicate. The letters were delivered on horseback. It took weeks to get a letter!

UNLOCK THE BIG ? I will know how communication and transportation have changed over time.

Vocabulary
....

communicate

e-mail   transportation

Communication Now

Today, we have faster ways to communicate Airplanes carry letters around the world. Now, it takes only a few days to get a letter.

We can use computers to communicate. An **e-mail** is a message sent through a computer. It takes seconds to get an e-mail!

We also use computers to connect to the Internet. We use the Internet to learn and work. We also use it to communicate.

1. **Underline** words that tell how we communicate today.

Transportation Then

Transportation is the way we move from place to place. Long ago, there were no cars or trains. People rode horses or walked to get from place to place. Some people rode in wagons pulled by horses. They traveled over water in small ships. It took months to travel a long way.

Transportation Now

Transportation is much faster today. We use cars, buses, and trains. We travel over water in large ships. We can fly in airplanes to visit places far away. Cars, trains, and airplanes are fast. Today, we can travel a long way in a day.

2.  **Main Idea and Details**
Circle the main idea in the paragraph above. **Underline** two details.

3. ◉ **Compare and Contrast** **Write** two ways people traveled in the past. **Write** two ways we travel today.

Past:

Present:

4. **What is one way that communication has changed from the past?**

my Story Ideas

⬛ **Stop!** I need help with _____

▶ **Go!** Now I know _____

Lesson 1

1. Draw a picture of something we use to measure time.

Lesson 2

2. Circle words that tell about time.

then	tomorrow	school
today	home	past
friends	now	present
long ago	future	clothing

3. ⊙ **Sequence Write** the word that comes next.

past, present, _____

4. Draw a line from each word to the correct picture.

photograph

document

5. Complete the sentence using words in the boxes.

hero	help

A _____ is someone who works to _____ others.

Lesson 5

6. Complete each sentence. **Write** one way life long ago was different from life today.

Long ago, ______________________

Today, ______________________

Lesson 6

7. Fill in the bubble next to the correct answer.
Which kind of transportation is used today to go far?

Ⓐ horse
Ⓑ wagon
Ⓒ airplane
Ⓓ bicycle

 **my Story Book**

Go online to write and illustrate your own **myStory Book** using the **myStory Ideas** from this chapter.

? How does life change throughout history?

Think about your travel back in time.

Draw something you "saw" in the past.

While you're online, check out the **myStory Current Events** area where you can create your own book on a topic that's in the news.

 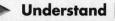 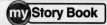

Atlas

The United States of America, Political

Washington
★Olympia

★Salem
Oregon

★Boise
Idaho

Montana
★Helena

North
Dakota
★Bismarck

South Dakota
Pierre ★

Wyoming

Carson
City★
Sacramento
★
Nevada

California

Salt Lake ★
City
Utah

Cheyenne
★

Denver ★
Colorado

Nebraska

Lincoln ★

Topeka ★
Kansas

Arizona

★Phoenix

Santa Fe
★

New
Mexico

Oklahoma

Oklahoma★
City

Texas

Austin
★

Alaska

Juneau ★

Honolulu
★

Hawaii

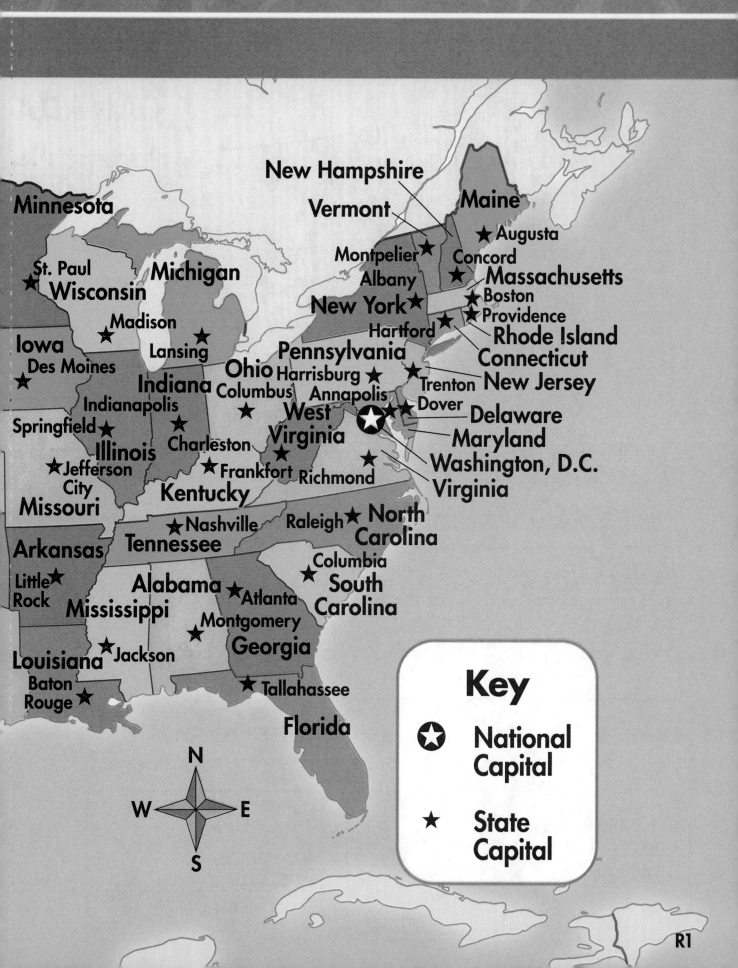

Minnesota

St. Paul ★
Wisconsin

Michigan

Madison ★

Lansing ★

Iowa
Des Moines
★

Indiana

Indianapolis
★

Springfield ★

Illinois

Jefferson ★
City

Missouri

New Hampshire

Vermont

Maine

★ Augusta

Montpelier ★
Concord
Albany ★

Massachusetts

New York ★
★ Boston

Hartford ★
★ Providence

Rhode Island

Connecticut

Pennsylvania

Ohio
Harrisburg ★

Columbus
Annapolis

West
Virginia

★ Trenton

New Jersey

★ Dover

Delaware

Maryland

Washington, D.C.

Virginia

Charleston

Frankfort ★

Richmond

Kentucky

Raleigh ★
North
Carolina

Nashville ★

Tennessee

Arkansas

Columbia
★ South
Carolina

Little ★
Rock

Alabama ★ Atlanta

Mississippi

Montgomery ★

Louisiana

Jackson ★

Georgia

Baton ★
Rouge

★ Tallahassee

Florida

N

W   E

S

Key

⭐ National
   Capital

★ State
  Capital

CANADA

Mt. Rainier

Rocky Mountains

Gannett Peak

Great Plains

Mt. Whitney

Mt. Elbert

PACIFIC OCEAN

Rio Grande

MEXICO

Mt. McKinley

0   400 mi

0   400 km

0   100 mi

0   100 km

Mauna Kea

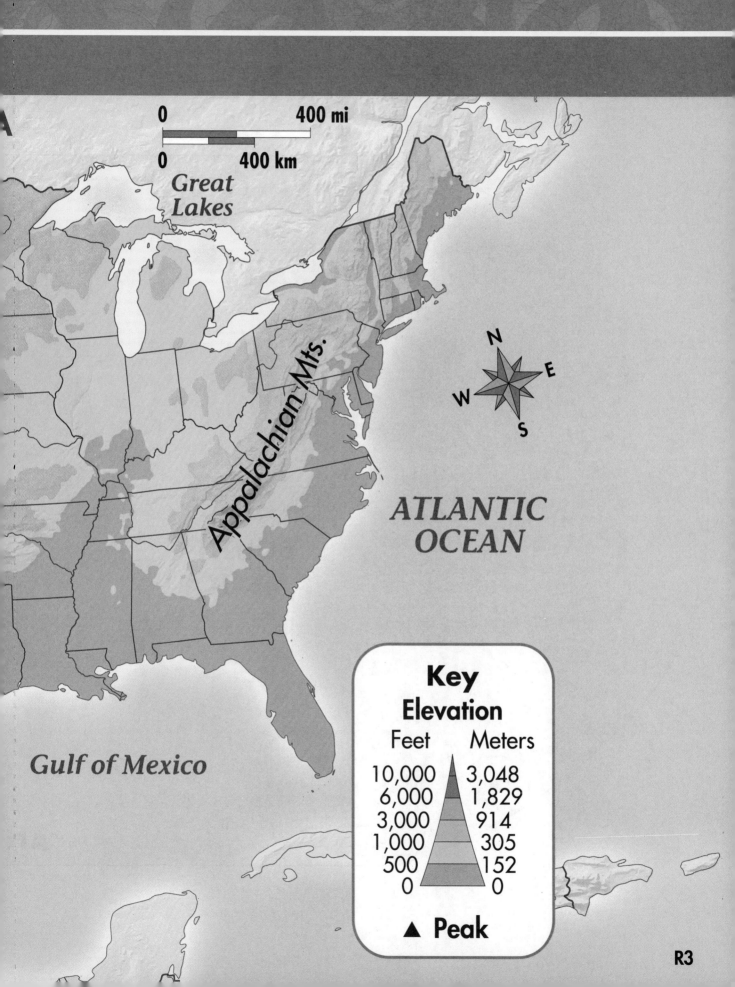

0

400 mi

0

400 km

Great
Lakes

Appalachian Mts.

N

W   E

S

ATLANTIC
OCEAN

Gulf of Mexico

Key
Elevation

Feet	Meters
10,000	3,048
6,000	1,829
3,000	914
1,000	305
500	152
0	0

▲ Peak

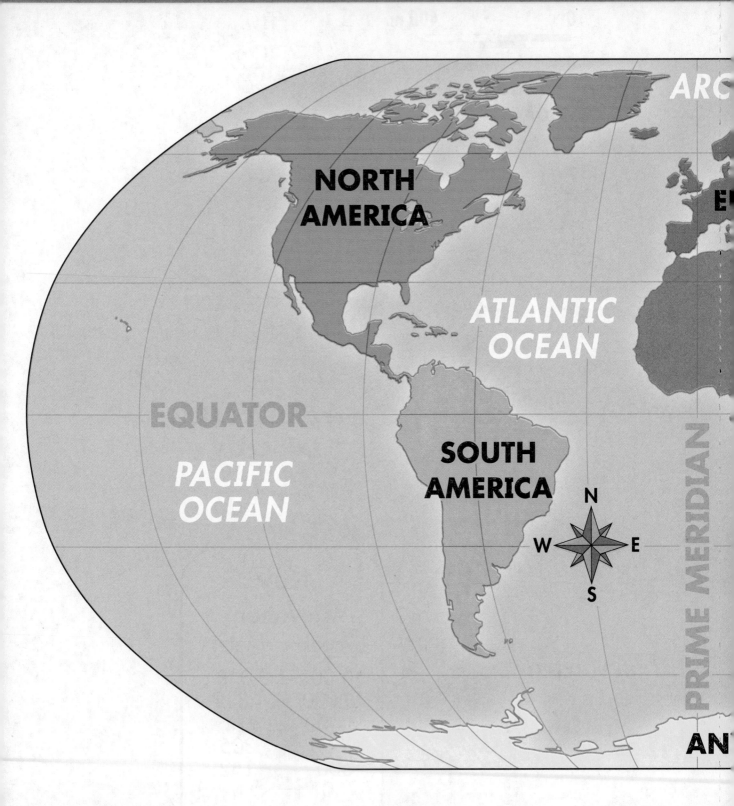

NORTH
AMERICA

ATLANTIC
OCEAN

EQUATOR

PACIFIC
OCEAN

SOUTH
AMERICA

ARC

E

PRIME MERIDIAN

AN

N
W   E
S

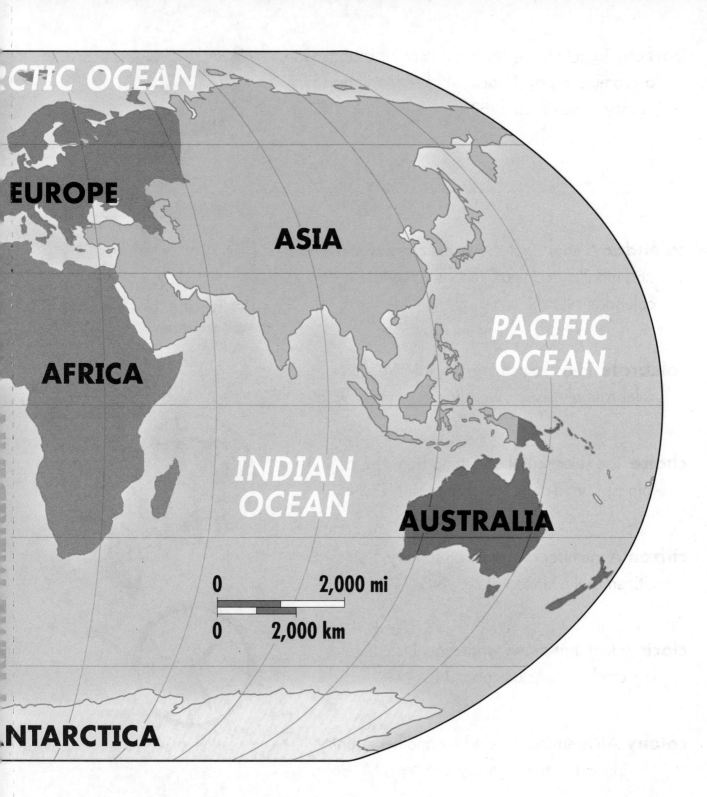

RCTIC OCEAN

EUROPE

ASIA

PACIFIC
OCEAN

AFRICA

INDIAN
OCEAN

AUSTRALIA

0   2,000 mi

0   2,000 km

NTARCTICA

Glossary

B

borrow To get money from a person or a bank with a promise to pay it back. My father will borrow money to buy a car. VERB

C

calendar A chart that shows the days, weeks, and months in a year. June is a month on the calendar. NOUN

celebrate To do something special. We will celebrate my sister's wedding tomorrow. VERB

choice The selection of one thing from two or more things. I have a choice of games. NOUN

citizen A member of a state or country. I am a citizen of the United States. NOUN

clock A tool that shows what time it is. There is a big clock in our classroom. NOUN

colony An area that is ruled by another country. Florida was once a colony of Spain. NOUN

Plymouth Colony

ATLANTIC OCEAN

Poor soil

Original Mayflower landing site

Plymouth

Cape Cod

Better farmland

communicate To share information with other people. People **communicate** by phone. VERB

community The place where people live, work, and play. My **community** has a parade on Memorial Day. NOUN

consumer Someone who buys goods and services. My mother is a **consumer** when she buys food. NOUN

continent A very large piece of land. North America is a **continent**. NOUN

cooperate To work together. We **cooperate** to keep the classroom neat. VERB

culture The way a group of people lives. Celebrating holidays is a part of **culture**. NOUN

custom The way people usually do something. It is a **custom** for people to shake hands when they meet. NOUN

D

desert A very dry area. A desert gets little rain. NOUN

direction A word that tells which way to go or where something is. South is one direction on a map. NOUN

document A paper with words on it. The Constitution is an important document. NOUN

E

electricity A kind of energy. Our lights use electricity. NOUN

e-mail Electronic mail, or a message sent through a computer. I got an e-mail. NOUN

explorer A person who travels to unknown places to find out what is there. An astronaut is an explorer. NOUN

F

fact Something that is true. It is a **fact** that George Washington was president. NOUN

family A group of people who live together. I have a large **family**. NOUN

fiction Something that is made up. The story of John Henry is **fiction**. NOUN

fiesta A public celebration with dancing and music. We will hear music at the **fiesta**. NOUN

future What will happen after today. I want to be a teacher in the **future**. NOUN

G

globe A model of Earth. I can find North America on a **globe**. NOUN

goods Things that workers make or grow. You can buy **goods** like shoes in this store. NOUN

government A group of citizens who work together to make rules and laws. Our state government passed a recycling law. NOUN

governor The leader of a state. Our governor wants us to help keep our parks clean. NOUN

H

hero Someone who works hard to help others. A firefighter is a **hero** who helps save lives. NOUN

hill A raised area of land, like a mountain but not as high. I live on top of a **hill**. NOUN

history The story of people, places, and events from the past. I study **history** in school. NOUN

holiday A special day. Kwanzaa is a **holiday** that my family celebrates. NOUN

I

invention Something that is made for the very first time. The light bulb was an important **invention**. NOUN

J

job The work people do. My **job** at home is to wash the dishes. NOUN

K

key A list of what symbols on a map mean. I used the map **key** to find the park. NOUN

L

lake A large body of water with land around it. We rowed a boat on the **lake**. NOUN

language The words we speak. My family speaks more than one **language**. NOUN

law A rule that everyone must obey. Our state has a **law** about wearing seatbelts. NOUN

leader Someone who helps people decide what to do. The mayor is a **leader** in my town. NOUN

M

map A drawing of a place that shows where things are. We used a **map** to find the way to your house. NOUN

market A place where goods are sold. My mother buys bread at the **market**. NOUN

mayor The main leader in a town or city. Ms. Garcia is the **mayor** of my town. NOUN

measure To divide something into parts that can be counted. We **measure** time in hours and days. VERB

money Coins or bills that people use to buy things. The game cost a lot of **money**. NOUN

mountain The highest kind of land. There is snow at the top of the **mountain**. NOUN

N

nation A group of people who have one government. The president is the leader of our **nation**. NOUN

needs Things that people must have to live. Food and clothing are **needs**. NOUN

O

ocean A large body of salt water. We swim in the **ocean** every summer. NOUN

P

past What has happened before today. I learned to ride a bike in the **past**. NOUN

present The time that is happening now. Schools are different in the **present** than they were in the past. NOUN

president The leader of our country. People vote to choose the **president**. NOUN

primary source Something written or made by a person who was at an event. A photograph is one kind of **primary source**. NOUN

producer Someone who makes or grows goods. A farmer is a **producer**. NOUN

R

recycle To make something new from something that has been used before. When we **recycle** paper, it can be made into new paper. VERB

reduce To use less of something. We can **reduce** the amount of water we use. VERB

responsibility Something people should do. Feeding our dog is my **responsibility**. NOUN

reuse To use something again. I **reuse** the same bag to carry things from the store. VERB

right Something that people are free to do or have. You have a **right** to attend school. NOUN

river A long body of water that often moves over land toward a lake or an ocean. We sailed our boat down the **river**. NOUN

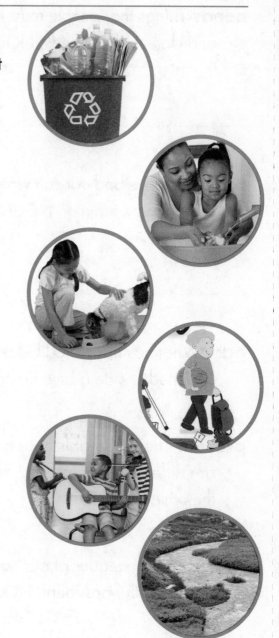

S

save To put money away to use at another time. I will **save** my money to buy the book. VERB

scarce Not enough of something. Most plants do not grow if water is scarce. ADJECTIVE

secondary source Something written or made by a person after an event happened. A history book is a secondary source. NOUN

services Work that people do for others. Teaching and coaching are services. NOUN

shelter A place to live. Everyone needs food, clothing, and shelter. NOUN

symbol Something that stands for something else. Our country's flag is a symbol of the United States. NOUN

T

trade To give something in return for something else. My friend and I like to trade books. VERB

trade-off Something you give up in order to get something else. The trade-off for playing soccer was having less time to read. NOUN

tradition A way to do something that people pass down over time. It is a **tradition** in my family to eat together on Sunday. NOUN

transportation The way people move from place to place. We use cars for **transportation**. NOUN

vote To make a choice that is counted. One day I will be able to **vote** for the president. VERB

wants Things we would like to have. Some of my **wants** are a game and skates. NOUN

weather What it is like outside at a certain place and time. I hope the **weather** is good for our picnic. NOUN

Index

This index lists the pages on which topics appear in this book. Page numbers in bold type show you where to find definitions.

Credits

Illustrations

CVR1, 22, 23, 29, 83, 119, 155 Nancy Davis; **CVR2, 24, 25** Dave Kirwin; **CVR2, 28, 29, 182** Jenny Matheson; **2, 3, 4, 5, 6, 7** Mary Anne Lloyd; **11, 18** Paul Eric Roca; **12, 62, 63, 64, 108, 109** Louise Ellis; **14, 48, 84** Viviana Garafoli; **32, 72, 156** Laura Huliska-Beith; **47, 86** Marcos Calo; **50, 51, 140, 141** Allegra Agliardi; **50, 96, 162** Shirley Beckes; **54, 58** Gwen Keraval; **68, 168, 169, FM** Holli Conger; **70, 86, 87, 104, 141, 142, 143** Bernard Adnet; **88, 114** Lyn Boyer; **90** Aga Kowalska; **120, 180** Nancy Cote; **130, 131, 178, 179** Karen Roy; **136** Steffane McClary; **161** Ivanke & Lola; **164** Marion Billett; **R7, R10, R15** Louise Ellis; **R8** Jenny Matheson; **R9** Bernard Adnet; **R9** Kory Heinzen; **R9** Viviana Garafoli; **R12** Marion Billett; **R13** Shirley Beckes.

Maps

XNR Productions, Inc.

Photographs

Photo locators denoted as follows: Top (T), Center (C), Bottom (B), Left (L), Right (R), Background (Bkgd)

Cover

CVR1 (CL) ©Associated Press, (BL) ©Free SoulProduction/Shutterstock, (BR) 1971yes/Shutterstock, (BCL) Comstock Images/AGE Fotostock, (TR) NPA/Stone/Getty Images, (BL) visuelldesign, 2010/Shutterstock; **CVR2** Jenny Matheson; **CVR2** (BL) ©DK Images, (C) Monkey Business Images/Shutterstock, (TR) Hulton Archive/Getty Images;

Front Matter

v (BR) Comstock Images/AGE Fotostock; **vi** (BL) Martin Wierink/Alamy; **ix** (BR) Rhea Anna/Getty Images;

14 (BL) Ariel Skelley/Blend Images/Getty Images; **15** (CR) Comstock Images/AGE Fotostock; **16** (B) David Young-Wolff/PhotoEdit, Inc.; **18** (B) ©DK Images; **19** (C) Wavebreakmedia/Shutterstock; **21** (TR) Frank Siteman/PhotoEdit, Inc.; **24** (BL) picturesbyrob/Alamy Images; **25** (CR) Karen Kasmauski/Terra/Corbis, (BR) Merrill Education; **28** (BL) Lacy Atkins/Corbis News/Corbis; **30** (TL) iStockphoto/Thinkstock; **31** (TR) Dennis MacDonald/PhotoEdit, Inc.; **32** (BL) Martha Asencio Rhine/Tampa Bay Times/ZUMA Wire/Alamy Stock Photo; **33** (BR) Stewart Cohen/Blend Images/Getty Images; **34** (BL) Christopher Halloran, 2010/Shutterstock; **35** (TR) Monkey Business Images/Shutterstock; **36** (C) henri conodul/Photolibrary Group, Inc.; **37** (C) Thomas Del Brase/Photographer's Choice RF/Getty Images; **38** (TR) David Madison/Getty Images, (BL) Jupiterimages/liquidlibrary/Thinkstock, (TC) Lagui, 2010/Shutterstock; **39** (CR) ©DK Images, (TC) Comstock/Thinkstock, (TL) Jupiterimages/Photos/Thinkstock, (BR) visuelldesign, 2010/Shutterstock; **40** (TL) Comstock/Thinkstock; **41** (TR) Rich Koele, 2010/Shutterstock; **51** (CR) IE127/Image Source/Alamy; **52** (B) Maria Spann/Getty Images, (TL) Ray Kachatorian/Getty Images; **54** (TC) Martin Wierink/Alamy, (TR) Roman Milert/Alamy; **56** (BL) iStockphoto/Thinkstock, (BR) Randy Faris/Corbis; **58** (BL) charlie bonallack/Alamy Images, (TC) Creatas Images/Thinkstock, (TL) Pixtal/SuperStock; **59** (TL) ©Masterfile Royalty-Free, (L) Peter Beck/Corbis, (TC) WoodyStock/Alamy Images; **60** (BL) Dave Nagel/Getty Images; **64** (TR) Hemera Technologies/Thinkstock; **66** (TL) Monkey Business Images/Shutterstock, (B) Ron Buskirk/Alamy Images; **68** (TC) Exactostock/SuperStock, (TR) Adempercem/Shutterstock; **69** (BR) Image Source/Getty Images, (TL) Pedro Nogueira, 2010/Shutterstock, (TC) Photos/Thinkstock; **74** (B) Jack Hollingsworth/Photodisc/Thinkstock, (TR) JLP/Jose L. Pelaez/Corbis; **75** (BC) Kevin Dodge/Corbis; **76** (TL) Shalom Ormsby/Blend Images/Corbis, (BL) Islandstock/Alamy Images; **78** (CL) Huw Jones/Alamy Images, (TL) Martin Wierink/Alamy, (TC) Pedro Nogueira, 2010/Shutterstock, (CR) Roman Milert/Alamy; **79** (BC) Monkey Business Images/Shutterstock, (BR) Pixtal/SuperStock; **90** (BL) Serg64, 2010/Shutterstock; **96** (BL) ©Jupiterimages/Thinkstock, (CL) Phil Emmerson, 2009/Shutterstock, (CL) Wendy Connett/Robert Harding World Imagery/Getty Images; **97** (BCR) ©DK Images, (B) Medioimages/Photodisc/Thinkstock, (TCR) Milosz Aniol, 2010/Shutterstock; **98** (B) Tischenko Irina/Shutterstock; **100** (TR) NPA/Stone/Getty Images; **104** (BR) Ariel Skelley/Blend Images/Corbis, (B) iStockphoto/Thinkstock; **105** (CR) iStockphoto/Thinkstock; **106** (BL) Corbis/SuperStock, (TL) Steve Smith/Purestock/SuperStock; **108** (BL) altrendo travel/Getty Images; **109** (CR) Vasca, 2010/Shutterstock; **110** (TR) Maksim Toome, 2010/Shutterstock, (B) Ocean/Corbis, (TC) Ssguy, 2010/Shutterstock; **111** (TL) EuroStyle Graphics/Alamy Images, (TC) iStockphoto/Thinkstock, (CR) Transtock/SuperStock; **112** (BL) Erin Patrice O'Brien/Photodisc/Getty Images, (T) moodboard/Corbis, (CL) Stockbyte/Thinkstock; **122** (CL) Bon Appetit/Alamy Images, (BL) Danny E Hooks, 2010/Shutterstock, (CL) Kai Wong/Shutterstock, (TC) NewsCom, (TR) VALERIE KUYPERS/AFP/Getty Images; **123** (BR) Masterfile Corporation; **124** (CL) David P. Smith/Shutterstock, (TL) gary yim/Shutterstock; **126** (TR) Creatas Images/Thinkstock, (BL) JGI/Tom Grill/Blend Images/Corbis, (TC) Sonya Stchison, 2010/Shutterstock; **127** (B) Ronnie Kaufman/Corbis; **128** (L) Atlantide Phototravel/Corbis; **130** (BL) ©Masterfile Royalty-Free; **132** (B) ©Lawrence Migdale/Getty Images; **134** (CR) Medioimages/Photodisc/Thinkstock, (CL) Tatjana Strelkova, 2010/Shutterstock; **136** (BL) Bob Adelman/©Magnum Photos; **137** (CR) Library of Congress, (BR) Ocean/Corbis; **138** (B) Thinkstock; **140** (BL) Hulton Archive/Getty Images; **144** (BL) Monkey Business Images/Shutterstock, (TR) Seiya Kawamoto/Thinkstock; **145** (CR) Steve Peixotto/Getty Images; **146** (BL) Cultura/Alamy, (TL) Hugh Sitton/Corbis;

148 (B) Nataliya Hora,2010/Shutterstock; **149** (B) iStockphoto/Thinkstock; **151** (TL) ©Masterfile Royalty-Free, (TR) JGI/Tom Grill/Blend Images/Corbis, (BL) Ocean/Corbis, (BR) Thinkstock; **152** (BL) Cultura/Alamy, (BR) Monkey Business Images/Shutterstock, (BC) Steve Peixotto/Getty Images; **154** (BL) Michael Brooks/Alamy Stock Photo; **158** (TR) Kevin R. Morris/Bohemian Nomad Picturemakers/Corbis; **159** (TL) Edwin Remsberg/Alamy Images; **164** (TR) View Stock/Alamy; **165** (BR) Monkey Business Images/Shutterstock, (TL) Everett Collection/SuperStock, (CR) Library of Congress; **166** (BL) Underwood & Underwood/Corbis; **167** (TR) TJ Brown/Shutterstock; **170** (TR) Darren Modricker/Corbis, (BL) Rhea Anna/Getty Images; **171** (CR) Bettmann/Corbis; **172** (TL) Gelpi, 2010/Shutterstock; **174** (BL) 1971yes/Shutterstock, (TC) Atlaspix/Shutterstock, (TR) Todd Strand/Independent Picture Service/Alamy Stock Photo; **175** (BR) Washington State Historical Society/Art Resource, NY; **176** (TL) ©Associated Press, (CL) Library of Congress, (BL) World History Archive/Alamy Images; **178** (CL) imagebroker/SuperStock, (BL) Kate Kunz/Corbis; **179** (CR) Edouard Debat-Ponsan/The Bridgeman Art Library/Getty Images, (BR) Monkey Business Images,2010/Shutterstock; **180** (BL) Ocean/Corbis; **182** (BL) Bettmann/Corbis, (BL) sequarell/Shutterstock; **183** (BR) ZouZou,2010/Shutterstock; **184** (CL) iStockphoto/Thinkstock, (TL) Nancy Carter/North Wind Picture Archives/Alamy Images; **187** (TR) Bettmann/Corbis, (CR) Underwood & Underwood/Corbis.

Glossary

R6 (TL) Shalom Ormsby/Blend Images/Corbis, (BR) Comstock Images/AGE Fotostock, (BL) Monkey Business Images/Shutterstock; **R7** (BR) NewsCom, (BL) Ronnie Kaufman/Corbis, (TL) Stockbyte/Thinkstock; **R8** (CL) Bettmann/Corbis, (BL) NASA, (TL) Wendy Connett/Robert Harding World Imagery/Getty Images, (BR) ZouZou,2010/Shutterstock; **R9** (CL) 1971yes/Shutterstock, (TR) Creatas Images/Thinkstock, (BL) Serg64,2010/Shutterstock, (CR) Steve Peixotto/Getty Images; **R10** (CR) ©Jupiterimages/Thinkstock, (CL) TJ Brown/Shutterstock, (TL) henri conodul/Photolibrary Group, Inc., (TCL) Hermera/Thinkstock, (BL) Kate Kunz/Corbis, (BR) Thinkstock; **R11** (CR) ©Lawrence Migdale/Getty Images, (TL) Dennis MacDonald/PhotoEdit, Inc., (BR) iStockphoto/Thinkstock, (CL) Milosz Aniol,2010/Shutterstock; **R12** (CL) Image Source/Getty Images, (TR) Jack Hollingsworth/Photodisc/Thinkstock, (BR) Phil Emmerson,2009/Shutterstock, (BL) Wally McNamee/Corbis; **R13** (CL) ©Christopher Halloran/Shutterstock, (CR) Monkey Business Images/Shutterstock, (BR) Darren Modricker/Corbis, (C) Library of Congress, (TL) Medioimages/Photodisc/Thinkstock, (BL) Pixtal/SuperStock; **R14** (TCL, BR) ©DK Images, (TR) Ariel Skelley/Blend Images/Corbis, (BL) Exactostock/SuperStock, (CL) Wavebreakmedia/Shutterstock, (TL) Mike Flippo/Shutterstock; **R15** (CR) David P. Smith/Shutterstock, (TCL) ©Masterfile Royalty-Free, (TR) Comstock/Thinkstock, (BR) Randy Faris/Corbis, (CL) Thinkstock; **R16** (TL) ©Masterfile Royalty-Free, (TR) EuroStyle Graphics/Alamy Images, (BL) IE127/Image Source/Alamy, (BR) Steve Smith / Purestock/SuperStock.